# CLASSIC BRITISH
# BIKES

## Abbeydale Press

First published in 2004 by Abbeydale Press
an imprint of Bookmart Ltd
Blaby Road, Wigston
Leicestershire, LE18 4SE, England

ISBN 1-86147-133-5

1 3 5 7 9 10 8 6 4 2

Originally published in 1997 by Bookmart Ltd
as *Classic British Bikes*, and in 1999 as
*The Handbook of Classic British Bikes*.

Production by Omnipress
Printed in Singapore

# Contents

Introduction............................4

## The Pioneers 1900 –1920

Introduction.................................6
Humber Trike.........................10
Matchless................................12
Triumph 3hp...........................14
P&M.........................................16
Singer......................................18
Norton 3$^{1}$/2hp.........................20
Wilkinson TMC.......................22
Ariel 3$^{1}$/2hp...........................24
Bat No.2..................................26
BSA 3$^{1}$/2hp............................28
Zenith Gradua........................30
Rudge Multi............................32
Triumph 3$^{1}$/2hp.......................34
Lea-Francis.............................36
Royal Enfield V-twin..............38
Scott 3$^{3}$/4 Two Speed.............40
Clyno......................................42
Douglas 2$^{3}$/4..........................44
Wooler....................................46

## Vintage Days 1920 –1940

Introduction............................50
ABC..........................................54
Levis Popular..........................56
Norton 16H............................58
Velocette Two-stroke.............60
Triumph Ricardo....................62
BSA Round Tank....................64

James V-twin...........................66
Brough Superior SS100..........68
Ner-a-car................................70
Cotton TT..............................72
Sunbeam Model 90.................74
Velocette KTT........................76
Norton CS1.............................78
Scott Squirrel.........................80
Matchless Silver Hawk...........82
Excelsior Manxman.................84
Norton International..............86
Vincent Rapide.......................88
Triumph Speed Twin 5T........90
BSA Gold Star.........................92
Rudge Ulster...........................94

## The Classic Era 1940 –1960

Introduction............................98
BSA M20................................102
Excelsior Welbike.................104
AJS 7R..................................106
Triumph GP & Trophy.........108
Vincent Rapide.....................110
Velocette KTT......................112
LE Velocette.........................114
BSA Bantam.........................116
Norton Model 18 & ES2......118
BSA A10 Golden Flash.........120
Royal Enfield Bullet.............122
Sunbeam S8..........................124
Vincent Black Prince...........126
Ariel Square Four.................128

Douglas Dragonfly.................130
Norton Dominator...............132
Velocette MSS.......................134
Norton International............136
BSA Gold Star.......................138
Triumph Tiger Cub...............140
Panther M120.......................142

## Endings & Beginnings 1960 –1997

Introduction.............................146
BSA C15T...............................150
Ariel Leader.............................152
Greeves Sports Twin...........154
Royal Enfield Constellation....156
Norton 500 Manx.................158
BSA A65..................................160
Velocette Thruxton.............162
BSA Rocket 3.........................164
Triumph T120 Bonneville......166
Norton Commando (Fastback)...168
Norton P11.............................170
Norton Commando (Roadster)...172
Triumph Trident....................174
Rickman Enfield Interceptor...176
Silk 700..................................178
Triumph T140 Bonneville......180
Hesketh Vampire..................182
Norton Rotary Wankel.......184
Triumph Trident....................186
Triumph T595 Daytona.........188
Triumph Thunderbird..........190

# Introduction

The motorcycle is little over one hundred years old. At the start of the 20th century it resembled a spindly motorised bicycle whose large but often unreliable engine offered a performance little better than a modern moped. By the end of the century, it had developed into a sophisticated and comfortable superbike, in some cases capable of sustaining speeds in excess of 150 mph for hours on end.

For well over 50 years, British bikes helped to force the pace of technological change, and for several decades could honestly claim to be the best in the world. British-built machines set speed records, won races and endurance trials, carried out seemingly impossible stunts – and carried their owners to work, day in, day out.

They were the favoured mounts of princes, film stars, industrialists, soldiers – and the ordinary working man and woman. They provided their owners with entertainment and freedom, kept the wheels of commerce turning, and played a major part in both world wars as well as many lesser conflicts. British motorcycle factories exported to half the globe – and the cousins of the machines that won races in Europe could be found earning their keep in rural communities across a British Empire that spanned almost every continent.

And then it all went wrong. In part the victim of increasing affluence, in part of mismanagement and shortsightedness, the British motorbike industry collapsed. In little more than 20 years it went from being the pride of the world to a half-forgotten footnote that owed its very existence to the dedication of a small band of enthusiasts.

Even so, the names of the great marques lived on: names such as BSA, Matchless, Norton, Sunbeam, and, above all, Triumph.

*The Handbook of Classic British Bikes* tells the story of the machines for which the label 'Made in England' was an international badge of pride.

*A century of progress has taken the motorcycle from its bicycle origins (left) to become a sophisticated high-performance machine (below). The history of the machines produced by the British motor cycle industry illustrates every step of that process.*

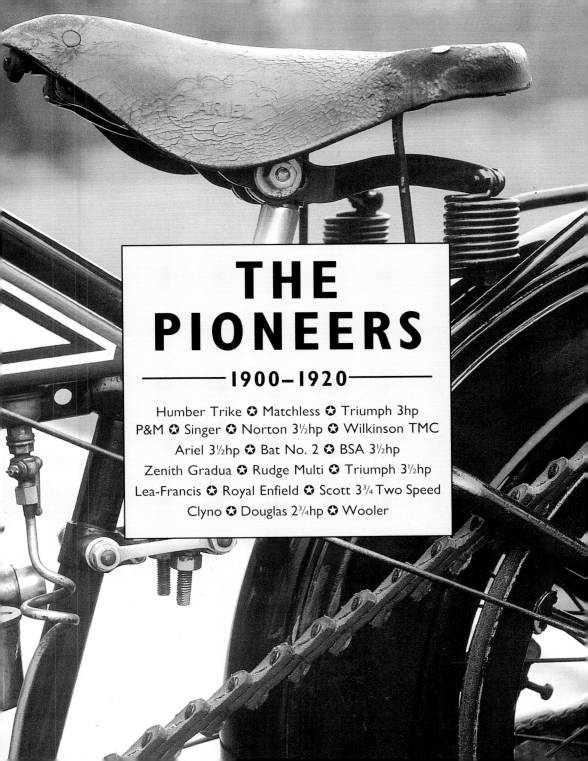

# THE PIONEERS

## 1900–1920

Humber Trike ✪ Matchless ✪ Triumph 3hp
P&M ✪ Singer ✪ Norton 3½hp ✪ Wilkinson TMC
Ariel 3½hp ✪ Bat No. 2 ✪ BSA 3½hp
Zenith Gradua ✪ Rudge Multi ✪ Triumph 3½hp
Lea-Francis ✪ Royal Enfield ✪ Scott 3¾ Two Speed
Clyno ✪ Douglas 2¾hp ✪ Wooler

# The Pioneers

No one can really say where the motorcycle began for it was the result of many simultaneous experiments in different countries.

Most historians date the motor industry from 1885 when two Germans Daimler and Maybach put the first really practical four-stroke engine into a wooden test vehicle that they called the Einspur. As it had two wheels albeit with a small pair of supporting wheels on each side this can be said to be the first motorcycle although Daimler and Maybach themselves saw it simply as a stepping stone to building the first car. But the British industry also got off to a flying start for, at around the same time, British inventor Edward Butler put forward his design for a twin-cylinder tricycle which in featuring electric ignition and a proper carburettor was in many ways more advanced than Daimler's. Sadly, ambitious plans to go into full production failed to materialise and Butler went no further than a prototype.

What is beyond dispute is that the German Hildebrand and Wolfmuller in 1894 was the first commercially successful motorcycle, while in France De Dion was building tricycles in 1895.

Unlike Europe, developments in Britain had been hampered by the Locomotive Acts of the 1860s which restricted speeds to less than a fast walking pace and were responsible for the notorious red flag that had to be carried in advance of any motorised vehicle. When this law was repealed in November 1896 it was the cause of celebrations that are commemorated to this day in the form of the London to Brighton Run.

The repeal helped a fledgling industry to get started, at first mainly through the efforts of established bicycle manufacturers eager to get to grips with the new technology. Most of them bought proprietary engines from the French manufacturers such as De Dion and Minerva while others obtained a licence to build machines.

*Before the turn of the century, would-be manufacturers had experimented with a host of alternatives. The forecar, an early attempt to accommodate a passenger within a tricycle layout, enjoyed a brief vogue.*

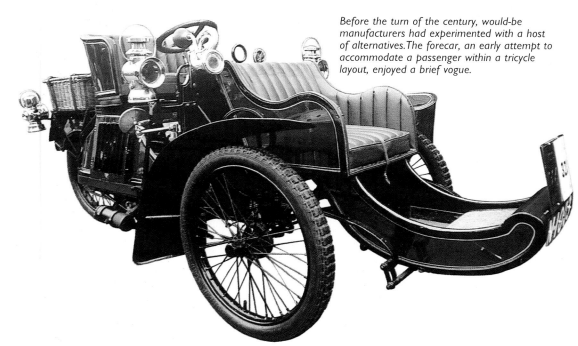

*The pioneer motor trade developed from the bicycle dealers and blacksmiths who had served an earlier generation. In 1913, Douglas dealer Frederick Turpin (above) also offered Scott, Clyno and Premier machines for as little as 25guineas. Almost 100,000 motorcycles were registered that year.*

There were many snags in getting the industry off the ground. Even if the basic design was sound – and many were not – public acceptance of the motorcycle was a long time coming. To start with, they were invariably expensive to buy and running costs were high. There were no wayside fuel stations and the road very often consisted of an unmetalled, rutted track covered with mud and horse manure. Speed traps were common, and there were many other legal restrictions on the pioneer motorist.

Unreliable, low-powered engines were the norm and this helped to delay the development of a proper motorcycle, since what was euphemistically termed 'light pedal assistance' was looked on as essential not only for starting but also for going uphill or even into a headwind. As a result, it was a long time before motorcycles dispensed with pedalling gear completely and became something other than motorised bicycles.

The need to retain the pedalling gear, as well as a natural desire to experiment, led to considerable debate about such matters as the location of the engine. There were many weird and wonderful alternatives, while the problem on the designer's mind was the dreaded 'side-slip' or skidding, a natural result of poor road surfaces, skinny tyres and what was often a very high centre of gravity.

It is perhaps surprising that the motorcycle evolved at all, but all the trials and tribulations must have been worth it for the occasional opportunity to fly effortlessly and unhindered down an open road.

The ingenuity and the enthusiasm of the designers knew no bounds, while the astonishing flexibility of the pioneering engines allowed them to triumph, despite the fact that most bikes lacked such items as a clutch or gearbox. Machines were generally started by a run and bump, and stalled when they stopped which initially limited their appeal to fit (and tall) young men.

Even so the fledgling British industry produced some astonishing designs including the world's first four-cylinder motorcycle. Development of the Holden began in 1896 and a water-cooled version was launched in 1899. With an engine that ran at just 400rpm and a power output of some 3bhp it completed a run of over 100 miles in 1900.

Such experiments apart it was clear for the most part that developments would centre on single-cylinder side-valve engines with simple air cooling.

It was not until the start of the 20th century that machines that were recognisably related to the modern motorbike became generally available on the British market. The French Werner helped to pioneer the conventional position of the engine in place of the bicycle's bottom bracket and many British manufacturers had their own variations on the theme. Although many of these early machines were too primitive and too demanding to appeal to anyone but committed and well-heeled enthusiasts the majority went surprisingly well and were also capable of turning in some astonishing speed and endurance records.

*Clearly displaying its bicycle origins, the layout of the motorcycle settled down in the early years of the 20th century. It became the convention to have the engine in the position of the bottom bracket, with a simple belt drive to a large rear-wheel pulley, as on this 1903 Kerry.*

*The sidecar developed as family transport, but soon found a new use on the battlefields of Europe, where the 'Trusty Triumph' single became the staple military machine.*

The problem of accommodating a passenger, which had led to strange inventions such as the trailer and forecar, was now resolved mainly by the equally odd sidecar. This, however, had the significant advantage that the passenger was separated from all the fuss and dirt of the motorcycle itself.

While road racing had helped developments in mainland Europe, British roads could not legally be closed for motor sport. As a result, many of the early speed races were undertaken on the banked tracks built as a result of the cycle boom, or on the driveways of private estates. But the bar to pure road racing was removed with the construction of Brooklands in Surrey, a banked road track designed by Holden, where the first full-scale motorcycle race was held in 1908. A year before, the Isle of Man, not subject to mainland restrictions, became the site of the first Tourist Trophy – effectively a cross between a race and a reliability trial – in 1907. Won at little over 36mph, it was a small beginning for a race that would become a dominant force in the British industry and then the world.

Before World War I, racing and commercial pressures had forced the pace of technological change, and most of the features of modern motorcycles had been tested in some form. Although the majority of machines still used a direct belt drive linking the engine and rear wheel, the advantages of a variable gear had been amply demonstrated, while numerous ingenious suspension systems had been tried. Chain drive, shaft drive, telescopic forks, four-valve engines, four-cylinder engines, water-cooled engines, overhead-camshafts and many other features recognisably similar to those of modern machines had all been seen – many of them British inventions. And with the outbreak of war the light manoeuvrable motorcycles produced by the leading British manufacturers found a host of applications which earned them respect in the most taxing conditions in history.

The following pages tell the story of legendary names such as BSA, Norton and Triumph – as well as the many machines that failed to survive those early pioneering days.

# Humber Trike

*Based on a pioneering French design the tricycle format of the Humber offered greater stability than a two-wheeler on the rough roads of the day.*

## Humber Trike (1898)

*Years in production:* 1898
*Engine type:* single-cylinder side-valve four-stroke
*Compression ratio:* 4:5
*Transmission:* direct gear drive to rear axle
*Top speed:* approx 40mph

Humber was established in 1868 by Thomas Humber, whose aim as a bicycle pioneer was to build the best quality machines possible at his works in Beeston, Nottingham. Although he quit the business in 1892, before it had any connection with powered transport, his bicycles had a fine reputation. In 1884, they pioneered the first diamond frame, a design that became universal for bicycles and formed the basis of most pioneer motorcycles.

During the cycle boom of the 1880s, Humber was built into a very large company indeed, with works in Beeston Coventry and Wolverhampton – because of its association with an English entrepreneur named Harry Lawson. At Lawson's behest, in 1896, Humber started work on a number of prototypes of an experimental machine. Although Humber and Lawson spent a great deal of money, none of the prototypes ever came to anything. The most promising was a version of a Humber tricycle that had a single rear wheel and passenger seat between two steerable front-wheels and a De Dion engine behind the rear wheel.

Harry Lawson's Motor Manufacturing Company (MMC) acquired the sole rights to the De Dion engine, which he built in Coventry. He also held the rights to the three-wheeler which he passed on to Humber in 1896.

In 1902, the firm acquired the rights to the P&M design and started to make this as the 'Humber Beeston'. They had also begun to experiment with their first cars which would prove even more successful. Humber continued to build motorcycles until 1930, and in 1911 even won the first Junior TT held over the Mountain Circuit. Some years later, motorcycle production ended as a result of the depression and the bicycle business was sold to Raleigh. But under the ownership of the Rootes group, the Humber name lived on for a century after the company was founded.

*The De Dion-based engine design (left) owed a great deal to pioneering Daimler, who made the first truly practical internal combustion engine. The aluminium alloy crankcase, radial finning and long holding-down bolts were De Dion innovations. Drive to the rear axle was by spur gear and pinion.*

# Matchless

Matchless was one of the true pioneers. Having become one of the first manufacturers in Britain, the firm really established themselves in 1907 by winning the single-cylinder class of the inaugural Isle of Man TT race. The company would go on to become one of the mainstays of the British industry.

Theirs was a familiar tale moving from bicycle manufacture to motor-cycle production although unlike most of their rivals they were not based in the Coventry or Birmingham area but in Plumstead, London. The firm was founded by H H Collier, whose young sons Harry and Charlie joined him before the end of the 19th century. Their first motorcycle had its French-made engine bolted under the front downtube of a bicycle-type frame. This appeared in 1899.

In 1902–3 their first production machines appeared. This machine used a 2³/4 hp De Dion engine manufactured under licence from the Motor Manufacturing Company (MMC).

Ignition and carburation were primitive, using a total-loss battery and coil arrangement and spray carburettor, but the models sold well enough to see further development, with an engine that was finally positioned in the centre of the frame ahead of the pedals.

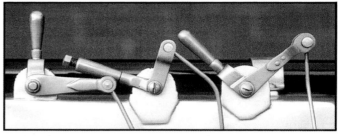

*Juggling act (above): early engines had few automatic functions, so a host of tank-top levers was necessary to keep the ignition and carburation on song.*

*The 1902–3 model (below) has its engine placed under the front downtube, but the Collier family experimented with a number of different layouts in the pioneering years.*

The inventive Colliers continued to experiment, and in 1904 launched a tri-car, with a pair of front wheels and single rear wheel. It was designed to provide transport for a passenger ahead of the driver between the wheels. The tri-car failed to sell well, and was dropped in 1905. But Matchless had already launched a new motorcycle that year, using the new V-twin engine built by fellow Londoner, J A Prestwich (JAP) of Tottenham.

Transmission was by the conventional direct belt, but where the model really showed the forward thinking of its makers was in its pioneering front and rear suspension. At the front it was by leading-link forks, while at the rear it consisted of a swinging fork with spring box under the saddle.

On such a model, Harry Collier represented Britain in an international race in France. The next year both he and his brother Charlie were entered, with Charlie coming third.

*The Collier name is cast into the crankcase of the side-valve V-twin. A three-speed hub gear is fitted, although there was a six-speed, that had a variable pulley and movable rear wheel.*

Charlie Collier won a famous TT victory in 1907, while Harry Collier recorded the fastest lap. They won again in the 1909 and 1910 TTs, while in 1908 a V-twin topped 70mph at the newly opened Brooklands racetrack. As World War I approached Matchless continued to develop their product. Surprisingly, they produced almost no motorcycles during the war, although the factory made an enormous contribution to munitions and aircraft. They went on to become one of the significant marques of the British industry.

*By the time that the 1912 V-twin (below) was built, motorcycle design had settled into a conformity – although on the way, Matchless had pioneered advanced suspension and many other features, including the dropped frame tube to lower the seating position.*

## Matchless 5hp V-twin (1912)

*Years in production:* 1912
*Engine type:* V-twin side-valve four-stroke
*Bore and stroke:* 85 x 85mm
*Compression ratio:* 4:1
*Capacity:* 770cc
*Transmission:* direct belt drive with three-speed hub gear
*Top speed:* approx 60mph

# Triumph 3hp

Like so many other pioneers, Triumph began as a bicycle company, founded in 1885 by a German expatriate, Siegfried Bettman. Together with a fellow German, engineer Mauritz Schulte, he set up in business in Coventry, choosing a company name that he believed would appeal to French and German buyers as well as the English.

That first Triumph motorcycle was designed in 1902 and used a proprietary Minerva engine in what was essentially a bicycle frame. The next, in 1903, had a JAP engine in a similar frame, but sales were slow, and Triumph decided that they needed to build their own power unit. Designed by Schulte in 1905, and backed by considerable commitment on Triumph's part, it was a simple side-valve single, using a much more advanced design. At a time when many rivals relied on inlet valves opened by suction, Triumph's was operated by a cam. The strong bottom end included proper main bearings, and a heavy flywheel to keep the engine running smoothly .

One of the key developments was a proper magneto. The early systems often relied on a coil and trembler powered by an accumulator or battery to provide a spark. As there was no charging system, the battery had to be recharged after a run. Some of the early Triumphs used this system but the 3hp offered the option of a magneto for the first time. Starting was improved and the rider was freed from reliance on a well-charged battery. The 3hp model still used a bicycle-type frame with direct drive to the rear wheel, but with rigid, braced forks, it was light and highly manoeuvrable. The next year, it gained a stronger frame and a primitive form of front suspension.

The engine was also improved, and in the first Isle of Man TT, held in 1907, J Marshall and F Hulbert took second and third place in the single-cylinder class. Sales took off, and reached a level of some 20 a week. From such simple beginnings, Triumph was on the way to becoming one of the major forces of the British motorcycle industry.

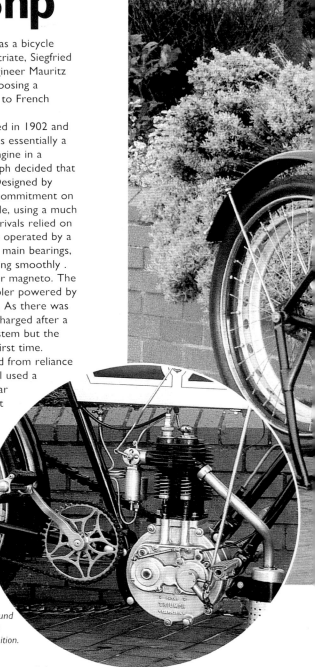

*The simple side-valve engine (right) would cruise at around 35mph and return a top speed of around 50mph for a miserly 90mpg. This model is equipped with battery ignition.*

### Triumph 3hp (1905)

*Years in production:* 1905-7
*Engine type:* single-cylinder side-
   valve four-stroke
*Bore and stroke:* 78 × 76mm
*Compression ratio:* 4:1
*Capacity:* 363cc
*Transmission:* direct belt drive
*Tyres (front/rear):* 2 × 22in/2 × 22in
*Wheelbase:* 49in
*Weight:* 125lb
*Top speed:* approx 50mph

*Little more than a heavyweight bicycle (around 125 lb) with a
363cc engine fitted ahead of the pedalling gear, the 3hp model
was the first true Triumph motorcycle. For its period, it was
remarkably advanced and reliable.*

# P&M

P&M was one of those firms that had a great idea and stayed with it for the next 66 years so that it effectively became the company's trademark. The great idea dated back to 1900, when Joah Carver Phelon went into business with Harry Rayner to develop a motorcycle. There was considerable debate about how to accommodate a motorcycle engine within the confines of a bicycle-type frame. Phelon's attractive solution was to remove the front downtube from the frame and fit the engine in its place. The engine was as strong as the tube, the centre of gravity was low, and the drive was conveniently positioned. More of Phelon's forward-thinking was evident in the choice of chain drive to the rear wheel, when almost all manufacturers opted for belts.

*The tank-mounted lever controls the two-speed gear.
Pulling it back engages the clutch connected to the low-ratio
sprocket pushing it forward engages the high-gear chain.*

Despite the machine's promise the Yorkshire-based company was tiny and had limited resources. Their first engines were fitted to frames made by Humber, but from 1902 the design was licensed to Humber themselves. In this form, the motorcycles achieving distinction in the 1902 RAC trials, using a 344cc engine with automatic inlet valve.

Phelon's original partner died in 1903, and in 1904 he went into a new partnership called Phelon and Moore, trademarked P&M of Cleckheaton, Yorkshire. They renegotiated the Humber licence to use the engine/frame design with a two-speed gear. The two-speed ratios used a pair of primary chains, engine sprockets and expanding clutches.

### P&M (1911)

*Engine type:* single-cylinder
    side-valve four-stroke
*Bore and stroke:* 84 x 89mm
*Capacity:* 498cc
*Transmission:* two-speed chain
    drive with expanding clutches

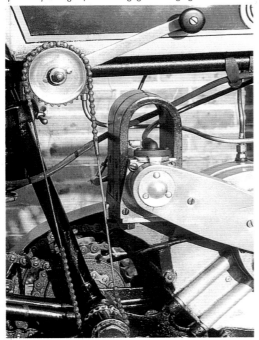

This enabled the drive to be disengaged which was a major advance in the days when most machines had to be bump-started. A patented half-compression device helped make starting easier. Mechanical inlet valves were introduced in 1910 with other refinements, but the two-speed gear remained.

P&Ms were the Royal Flying Corp's model of choice in World War I. Civilian production of a similar machine returned in the 1920s and in 1926 the trademark 'Panther' was adopted. But right up to the the time the last motorcycle left the Cleckheaton works in the 1960s, it still used its engine in place of the front downtube.

*The steeply inclined engine runs from headstock to bottom bracket of the frame, in place of the normal downtube. As well as having strong castings, high tensile steel rods run the length of the engine to provide additional stiffness.*

*P&M's original design dated to a time when manufacturers were still undecided about where to put the engine. Such was their foresight that it helped to establish both their own firm and Humber, while the addition of a workable two-speed gear in 1904 again put them well ahead of the competition.*

# Singer

Based in Coventry, Singer first made a name for themselves with a product called the Singer Motor Wheel. This was a novel idea first developed before the end of the 19th century, when solutions to the problem of where to put the engine in a pedal cycle frame were being sought. The motor wheel was the brainchild of a company called Perks and Birch who patented it in 1899. It included a complete engine with tank and transmission built inside a wheel that would fit into the rear forks of an ordinary bicycle.

Singer, already makers of bicycles and tricycles, took over the patent and refined the design. Fitted to the rear wheel of a bicycle or the front wheel of a tricycle it became popular at once and sold well. Simple to operate, the 208cc engine had a single speed control lever fitted to the handlebars. The ignition used probably the first effective motorcycle magneto. The pedalling gear of the bicycle was left in place so that the rider could use it for starting,

*Pioneer ergonomics dictated placing the controls where it suited ease of manufacture (left). Levers fitted to the tank were not necessarily easy for the rider to operate, but with little traffic, it was possible to take time to make running adjustments.*

and for the 'light pedal assistance' that most of the pioneer motorcyclists were expected to provide on hills.

Singer had always made all the components themselves and after 1904 it was a short step to making a motorcycle of more conventional appearance. This was similar to well-established contemporary designs, such as the Triumph, and placed a single-cylinder engine centrally in front of the pedalling gear of the bicycle, using direct belt drive to the rear wheel. The magneto moved to the front of the engine and carried a distinctive external horseshoe magnet. With its flat tank, its pepperpot silencer and strutted, braced girder forks this was almost the archetypal pioneer layout. Several variations on the theme appeared including 350cc two-strokes and later water-cooled four-strokes. The most popular were the conventional air-cooled side-valves of 299, 499 and 535cc.

Meanwhile the Singer car had developed from early experiments with three-wheelers and by World War I had become the company's mainstay. After several mergers, the Singer name lived on in the British car industry until the 1960s, long after the motorcycles were forgotten. As for the Singer Wheel, an almost identical concept made a brief resurgence in the years after World War II as part of the cyclemotor boom – with the BSA Winged Wheel as perhaps the best known. A similar engine in the wheel even appeared as a Honda moped of the 1960s.

*Light, but sturdy. Singer's machines were beautifully engineered by a company that made all of their components in-house.*

## Singer (1911)

*Years in production:* 1904–15
*Engine type:* single-cylinder
  side-valve four-stroke
*Capacity:* 299cc
*Compression ratio:* 5.5:1
*Gearbox:* direct belt drive
*Wheels and tyres:* 26in x 2½in
*Top speed:* approx 45mph

# Norton 3½hp

Few individual machines become so famous as to acquire their own nickname. But the Norton 3½hp, called 'Old Miracle', amply justified its name, with over 100 records and a performance that, with a top speed in excess of 80mph was hardly to be credited from an unsophisticated belt-drive single.

The first Nortons were made in 1902, the product of James Lansdowne Norton, bicycle fittings manufacturer of Birmingham. The first machine to bear his name used an imported clip-on engine; it was effectively a power-assisted bicycle. However, a subsequent machine was powered by a V-twin Peugeot engine aboard which H Rem Fowler won the prestigious twin-cylinder class of the first-ever Isle of Man Tourist Trophy in 1907, and set the fastest lap.

It was partly in response to this famous victory that Norton began to build his own engines, starting at the 1907 Stanley Show with his Model No.1 the Big Four. A 633cc side-valve single it would continue in production (albeit heavily updated) until 1954. In 1909, Norton introduced a smaller version. Rated at 3½hp, it was actually of 475cc with 82 x 90mm bore and stroke. A new 490cc model appeared two years later for the 1911 Senior TT races, that would grace Nortons for a further 50 years. Again called the 3½, it would grow into the Model 16 and then the 16H.

The new model began setting records. In 1911, Dan Bradbury was the first rider of a machine under 500cc to top 70 mph, while in 1912, Jack Emerson won the 150 mile Brooklands TT by some 13 minutes, setting a string of records in the process.

Simplicity was the key to Norton's success. The circular crankcase contained full-circle flywheels and a substantial big-end. The head and barrel were cast in one but had substantial finning and a good clear passage for cooling air with a simple sweep of the exhaust pipe providing the most efficient path for the emerging gases. The rest of the machine followed the normal Norton

*Simplicity characterises the engine (left), with smooth surfaces and easy curves. Rugged construction, plus the easiest possible passage for the gas and a cooling airflow are the secrets of its performance and reliability.*

*Simplicity as an art form. The length of the frame emphasises the spareness of the lay-out, consisting of little more than engine, drive belt and the lightest possible cycle parts.*

*The tyre inflator atop the flat tank is a reminder of the hazards of pioneer motorcycling (right).*

pattern of long, low-frame, girder forks and flat tank. The handling was legendary. Norton started to use the slogan 'The Unapproachable', which stayed with the company down decades of racing success. In 1913 Norton advertised themselves as holding seven world records, including the mile at over 73mph. When war intervened production went into temporary abeyance. Although the Norton 3½hp was resurrected in 1919, it was as the Model 16 that the next part of its story would be written.

## Norton 3½hp (1911-14)

*Engine type:* single-cylinder
   side-valve four-stroke
*Bore and stroke:* 79 x 100mm
*Capacity:* 490cc
*Tyres (front/rear):* 2½in clinchers
*Brakes:* rim
*Top speed:* 80+mph

# Wilkinson TMC

Wilkinson's luxurious four-cylinder touring motorcycle must surely have been the most sophisticated machine of its age – and the most comfortable including front and rear suspension and a car-type upholstered seat. The product of the prestigious Wilkinson Sword Company it was engineered to the highest quality and had a design that was years ahead of its time.

Wilkinson had dabbled with a proprietary single-cylinder engine machine as early as 1903. However, in 1908, a young designer, P G Tacchi, had patented a design for a military scouting motorcycle equipped with a Maxim machine gun. As military suppliers, Wilkinson were attracted by the scheme, and despite their failure to win an army contract they decided to persevere.

The Tacchi design used a proprietary V-twin engine and forks, but in other respects including the rear suspension, it resembled the Wilkinson that followed. The Touring Auto-Cycle (TAC) was introduced in 1909 and was aimed at the civilian touring market.

Powered by a 676cc four-cylinder air-cooled engine it featured a car-type clutch and three-speed gearbox plus shaft drive. There was a new fork design by Tacchi which used quarter-elliptic leaf springs as at the rear. Steering was either by long, swept-back handlebars, or a car-type steering wheel. After an enthusiastic reception, production began at Wilkinson's works in West London. A couple of years later there was a major change to the design with the launch of the Touring Motor Cycle (TMC).

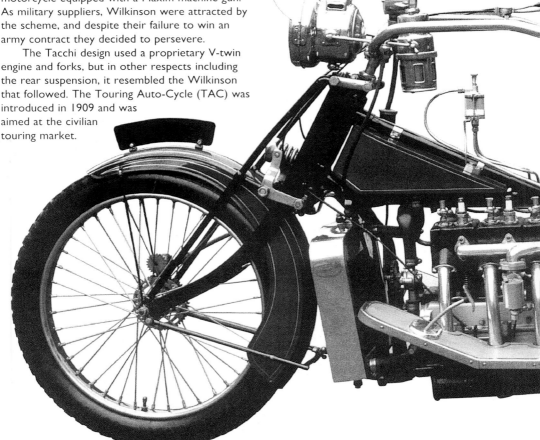

The massive Jones speedometer is positioned for maximum visibility.

The most obvious alteration was the use of a water-cooled side-valve engine, now of 848cc. There was also a return to a more conventional type of proprietary front fork.

In fact there were many changes throughout the development of the Wilkinson, which was hand-built in small numbers. A larger 996cc engine was offered in 1913, mainly for the potential sidecar user.

World War I, and the rise in demand for arms, meant that Wilkinson suspended production. But rights to the TMC and a light car that Wilkinson had also been working on were taken over by Ogston another West London firm. When peace returned, Ogston concentrated their efforts on the car, while Wilkinson turned the factory over to making garden tools . Only a couple of hundred Wilkinson fours had ever been made, but their demise spelt the end to one of the most interesting pioneers of the British industry.

## Wilkinson TMC (1909-16)

*Engine type:* four-cylinder water-cooled side-valve four-stroke
*Bore and stroke:* 60 x 75mm
*Capacity:* 848cc
*Transmission:* car-type three-speed gearbox and shaft drive
*Carburettor:* Stewart Precision
*Suspension:* Saxon front forks, quarter-elliptic rear springing
*Top speed:* approx 50mph

*Luxuriously equipped and sophisticated, Wilkinson's four-cylinder machines were dubbed the 'two-wheeled Mercedes' but were only ever hand-built in small quantities.*

# Ariel 3½hp

A chain-driven magneto and a float carburettor were two features that kept Ariel ahead of competitors.

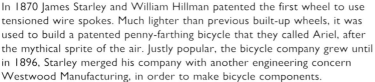

In 1870 James Starley and William Hillman patented the first wheel to use tensioned wire spokes. Much lighter than previous built-up wheels, it was used to build a patented penny-farthing bicycle that they called Ariel, after the mythical sprite of the air. Justly popular, the bicycle company grew until in 1896, Starley merged his company with another engineering concern Westwood Manufacturing, in order to make bicycle components.

The first motorised Ariel came two years later, in the form of a quadricycle, or quad, effectively a four-wheeled bicycle using a French De Dion engine driving the rear axle. This was soon modified into a motor tricycle based on the De Dion design but with improvements which carried the engine nearer the centre of the frame. Carefully designed and constructed the tricycles sold well.

The first Ariel motorcycles appeared in 1902, and were ahead of most of the competition using an engine manufactured by Kerry, with proper carburettors and magneto ignition, at a time when hit-or-miss hot-fuse ignition was the norm.

The company was called Components Ltd, run by Charles Sangster. In 1905, Ariel was chosen by the Auto Cycle Club (ACC) to represent Britain in the International Cup Races. Rider J S Campbell won the event at an average speed of over 40 mph. Other early stunts included the 'end-to-end' run from John O'Groats to Lands End.

Even so, sales were slow; more a reflection of the high price of a motorcycle in general – then around a year's wages for the average worker – than any product failings. Models with 2 and 3½hp engines were on offer at £25 and £50 respectively.

## Ariel 3½hp (1913)

*Years in production:* 1913
*Engine type:* single-cylinder
   side-valve four-stroke
*Bore and stroke:* 85 x 88mm
*Capacity:* 499cc
*Transmission:* direct belt drive
*Top speed:* 55mph

In 1910, Ariel launched a new model with a powerful 4hp side-valve engine built by White and Poppe. This was such a sound design that it was still in service in 1925.

By the start of World War I, the range included a 500cc side-valve engine and a 6hp V-twin, and a lightweight 350cc two-stroke. Despite advanced ideas, the war put paid to these promising designs. However, a number of Ariel motorcycles saw armed service, and by the end of the conflict, the company was well-positioned to take advantage of the post-war boom.

*Solidly conventional, the Ariel solo was well engineered and set enviable standards of reliability, helping the marque to be one of the industry's leading names.*

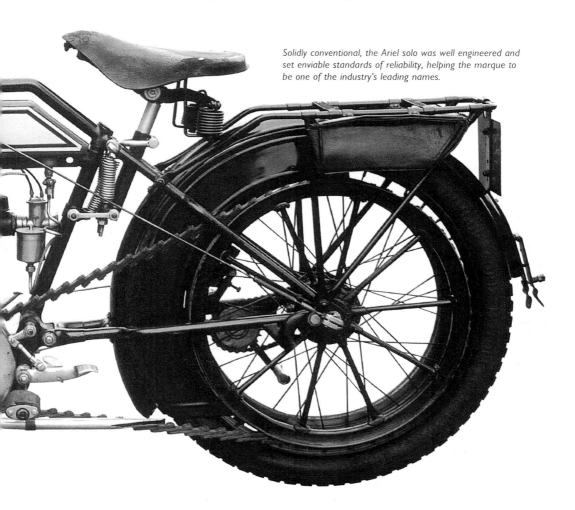

# Bat No. 2

Among the early British pioneers, Bat was perhaps the first to make a serious effort to exploit the publicity available from racing and record-breaking. But their impact was much deeper than this, for the firm produced some of the most technically sophisticated machines of the era, setting standards that others were soon to follow.

The company, based in Penge, South London, was founded in 1902 by a Mr Batson, after whom the bikes were named. The company's Model No.1 was built using a 2¾hp De Dion engine, and although it was basically a sound product, poor sales resulted in the founder selling the company within two years to Theodore Tessier, a very able rider. From the outset, Bat motorcycles showed their maker's desire to advance the state of motorcycle engineering, dispensing with the pedalling gear, fitting a clutch and patenting a fully sprung suspension system. The saddle and footrests were carried on the subframe, which was also suspended on springs.

Sales began to boom after Tessier took over, partly because of the quality of the product, but also because Tessier was skilled publicist. Launching a single cylinder 3½hp model in his first year, he set about racking up a score of over two hundred wins and speed records. V-twin machines using engines supplied by the Tottenham firm JAP followed, with 650, 770, 964 and 980cc power units fitted. Tessier rode a Bat in the very first Isle of Man TT in 1907, and although it failed to place, the next year's Bat entrant W H Bashall took a second in the twin-cylinder class. Bashall also scored the lap record of 42.25mph. Two years later, in 1910, H H Bowen upped this to 53.15mph – but although Bats were regularly entered prior to World War 1, this would be the last time they entered the TT record book. Reliability was probably their great weakness, for they were technically very competent and of proven high performance.

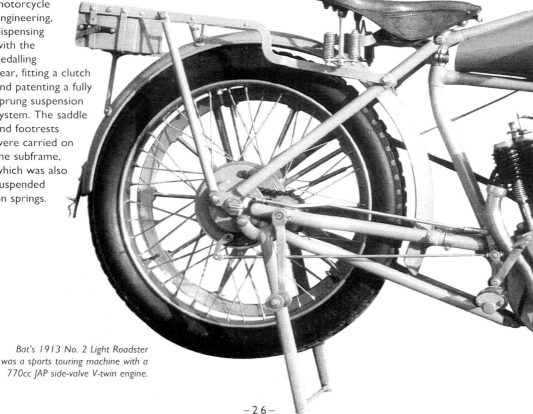

Bat's 1913 No. 2 Light Roadster was a sports touring machine with a 770cc JAP side-valve V-twin engine.

*Short leading-link forks were a Bat hallmark from the early days. The principle was similar to that employed by later makers such as Greeves, half a century later.*

The year 1911 saw the introduction of the mountain section at the TT, in response to which manufacturers, including Bat, began fitting gearboxes. Bat offered a two-speed unit as an alternative to the direct belt drive used previously. Both systems were then used in parallel for two years.

By 1913, Bat machines had become more conventional. The spring frame was dispensed with and models had a combination of gearbox and belt drive to the rear wheel.

World War I then intervened, and contrived to dent Bat's fortunes over some machines supplied to the Russian army, for which they were never paid. This left Bat in a poor position to fully exploit the post-war demand for cheap motorcycle transport.

Even so, Bat were in a much better position than the fledgling Martinsyde company, which built its first machines in 1919, but foundered in 1923. Bat took over the company and started to sell Bat-Martinsydes for the next three years. Finally, underfunded, and in the face of too much competition, Bat itself succumbed to the inevitable in 1926, after almost a quarter century in which they helped to establish the motorcycle in its modern-day form.

## Bat No. 2 (1913)

*Engine type:* V-twin side-valve four-stroke
*Bore and stroke:* 72 x 78mm
*Capacity:* 770cc
*Compression ratio:* 5.5:1
*Top speed:* approx 75mph

# BSA 3½hp

*The vintage side-valve displays typical concern for easy valve replacement. Removable caps over the valve heads made it simple to deal with a decoke or a broken valve stem, although the shape of the cast-iron cylinder made it a complex casting.*

The company that was to become Britain's largest motorcycle factory was rather late getting started in the new industry. But when they put their first machine on the market, its shrewd combination of the best features pioneered by others helped it to establish a reputation for quality and reliability that formed a solid foundation for BSA's later fortunes.

The Birmingham Small Arms (BSA) was originally a gunmaker's trade association with its roots dating back three hundred years. The BSA company proper was founded in 1861, and made guns for the next 20 years until they took up with the new bicycle industry in 1880. Then the outbreak of the Boer War meant an increased demand for guns and bicycle manufacture was shelved until peace offered a new market.

During the early years of the century many of BSA's fellow bicycle manufacturers enthusiastically launched their pioneer motorcycle designs, with BSA as a supplier of parts. BSA experimented with a proprietary engine, in 1905, fitted into one of their bicycle frames, but not until 1909 did they seriously develop their own product.

In 1910, they launched their 3½ hp belt-driven single. By this time, the early experimentation had settled down and it was clear to BSA that this type of machine was by far the most popular, particularly in the form of the contemporary Triumph – which was already well-established as a practical all-rounder. The new BSA offered a number of advantages from the outset over the Triumph, which the firm proceeded to improve on. The simple side-valve engine was very close to the Triumph design. But in 1913, BSA started to use a désaxé design in which the cylinder is mounted ahead of the crank axis, resulting in smoother running and less wear.

*The racing form of the early BSA dispensed with such touring concessions as the pedalling gear – which was fitted behind the engine – for the ordinary road rider. Its dropped frame tube and lowered saddle anticipated such a move by many of its rivals.*

The frame was conventional and clearly based like its contemporaries on pedal cycle technology. But in 1912 the top tube was bent down behind the tank giving a lower seating position -- a fashionable, practical change in which BSA preceded Triumph by a year or so. Where they scored a real mark over their rivals, however, was in the use of a parallelogram-type front fork with a cantilevered spring – a vastly better suspension system than that offered by other makers – notably the infamous Triumph fore-and-aft pivoted design.

The model sold well until World War 1, and was joined by a larger version aimed at the sidecar market. This became the basis of a military model and together with a huge demand for munitions helped BSA to grow almost four-fold by 1918 when it was ideally positioned to exploit the post-war boom.

## BSA 3½hp (1913)

*Years in production:* 1910–14
*Engine type:* single-cylinder
  side-valve four-stroke
*Bore and stroke:* 85 x 88mm
*Capacity:* 499cc
*Carburettor:* BSA
*Tyres (front/rear):* 2¼in x 26in/
  2¼in x 26in
*Wheelbase:* 55in
*Top speed:* 50mph

# Zenith Gradua

Among the machines favoured by sporting riders before World War I, Zenith machines fitted with the factory's Gradua gear were among the first to offer a really practical variable drive ratio. For a few years they were so successful in hill-climbs and other early events that they were barred from single-gear competitions. The company took this as a compliment and even added the word 'Barred' to their badge.

The earliest pioneer machines relied on direct belt drive to the rear wheel. Although their engines were designed for maximum flexibility, the fixed gear that resulted meant that a machine that could

start off and pull up hills easily would have had a severely limited top speed. The alternative adopted by early sporting riders was to use an adjustable pulley which could be opened to give a smaller effective diameter, and hence a higher gear. The only problem this posed, was that the belt tension was lost and it had to be shortened to suit. One early rider's manual devoted two pages to the process of climbing a hill and a similar amount to descending at speed afterwards.

Zenith changed all that with a belt drive system, the ratio of which could be varied on the move. Although technically limited, it was good enough to

*Zenith manufactured a wide range of machines using the Gradua system. Some versions adopted a chain-cum-belt drive, with a short chain to a separate pulley in front of the engine, as seen on this 1914 V-twin.*

The flanges of the front pulley (left) are opened and closed to give a smaller or larger effective diameter.

Belt tension is adjusted by moving the rear wheel back and forth, controlled by the bevel gears (right) at the base of the shaft.

ensure the marque's success in many important competitions and having demonstrated the virtue of variable gearing it paved the way for even more practical alternatives.

Zenith was established in 1904 in Stroud Green, North London. Like most pioneers, they used proprietary engines, fitted to a bicycle-type frame

with direct belt drive. But in 1908, designer Freddie Barnes developed the variable engine pulley. This had a pair of flanges that could be moved in or out by winding a handle while the machine was on the move. There were a number of limitations to this device. Unlike the chain drive that would eventually take over, belts were prone to slip in the wet, while the limited gear ratios still needed a large, flexible engine to make the best use of them. But with the JAP V-twins fitted to the majority of early Zeniths the theoretical limitations were overcome.

Improvements to the Gradua system followed including a variation in which a chain transmitted power to a gearbox forward of the engine. Transmission from there on was by Gradua belt drive.

Zenith continued in production from a new site in South London, making machines powered by everything from a lightweight Villiers-powered two-stroke single to a 1100cc side-valve V-twin. Post-war, they restarted with a 750cc V-twin but in 1950 ceased production mainly because of the lack of suitable proprietary engine makers.

### Zenith Gradua

*Years in production:* 1908–20
*Engine type:* single-cylinder or V-twin side-valve four-strokes

The 1912 model (below) used a JAP engine single-cylinder side-valve engine by J A Prestwich of Tottenham, North London.

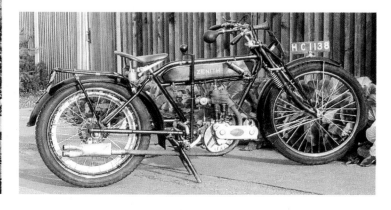

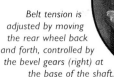

# Rudge Multi

## Rudge Multi (1913)

*Years in production:* 1912–23
*Engine type:* single-cylinder inlet
   over exhaust four-stroke
*Bore and stroke:* 85 × 88mm
   (3.5hp) 85 × 132mm (5/6hp)
*Capacity:* 499cc, 750cc
*Carburettor:* Senspray
*Tyres (front/rear):* 2¼in × 26in
   2¼in × 26in
*Top speed (racing model):* 83mph

Produced by one of Britain's foremost makers, the Rudge Multi was not just a single motorcycle but a new concept, which was an important stage in the development of motorcycle transmission systems, superseding the equally influential Zenith Gradua. Launched in 1912, after the 1911 TT had shown the value of its multiplicity of drive ratios, it remained in production for 10 years.

Founded in the 1860s by Dan Rudge, a publican from Wolverhampton and a keen racing cyclist, Rudge bicycles had patented numerous technical advances and established a name for quality by the time Rudge died in 1880. The firm was kept going through various mergers, and by the end of the 19th century, after a merger with the Whitworth company in 1894, was producing 400 bicycles a day, under the guidance of Charles and John Pugh.

Rudge Whitworth started by distributing Werner motorcycles from Paris, and it was 1909 before they undertook development of their own motorcycles. They were soon making some 1500 machines a week, and had the in-house resources to undertake all the development.

The Rudge Multi prototype had several patented features, including a new fork shackle, enclosed fork spring and a removable rear mudguard. The engine was a compromise between a side-valve and an overhead-valve, known as an F-head, but the machine was otherwise conventional.

The first Rudge motorcycle was completed in 1910, in just under two weeks from drawing to metal. Following many road tests and competitions, the model went on sale at the end of the year.

In 1911, four Rudges started at the Senior TT, the first year in which the course included the climb over the Mountain. By this time, experiments with proprietary variable gear pulleys made by Mabon had proved the value of such a device on the demanding new course. However, Rudge's first efforts at the TT were not so promising, with two riders retiring, and only a 21st and 22nd place.

Nevertheless, convinced of the value of a variable gear, John Pugh continued development of what was to be the Multi system. Rudge had already patented a clutch that was attached to the engine shaft, outboard of the pulley. To this was added a device that allowed the pulley flanges to open and close. As it did so, the belt would ride up the pulley, changing the effective diameter of the drive.

*Patented fork shackles and an enclosed fork spring were Rudge features that would endure for many years.*

To maintain belt tension, a linkage went to the rear wheel pulley, or belt rim, which closed and opened to balance the front. This gave ratios between 3.5 and 7.5:1, as well as in theory, continuously variable selection.

Fitted to the 499cc TT model the Multi was first entered for the 1912 TT. Although Rudge failed to place, the Multi gear achieved successes at

*The tall, exceptionally long stroke engine gains even greater height as a result of its use of an overhead inlet valve – the 'F-head' arrangement (right).*

*Appearing on a 1913 model of 750cc, the Rudge Multi (below) soon became renowned for its advantage in speed trials and racing, as well as for the average rider.*

numerous trials and speed events, and was fitted to both the 3.5hp and 5/6hp models. In 1913, a Rudge Multi took second place at the TT, losing only by a narrow margin, and in 1914, Cyril Pullin won the event. During World War I, Rudge built a few machines for military use, but the main part of the factory was turned over to work on munitions. When peace returned, so did motorcycles, starting with the 499cc Multi in Roadster or TT form. In 1920, the first Rudge to use a three-speed gearbox appeared, but the Multi was in production until 1923, its cheap, simplicity and lightness appealing long after the technical superiority of chain drive and a countershaft gearbox had been proven.

# Triumph 3½hp

Triumph's pioneering 3½hp (500cc) models did more than any other machine to influence the mass acceptance of the motorcycle. Certainly Triumph were one of the first to undertake mass production on a really major scale and the reliability of their early models led to their later machines becoming known as Trusty Triumphs.

By 1907, Triumph's solidly engineered 3hp singles had gained the company a good reputation as makers of reliable machines with a fair turn of speed. Part of that reliability came from the Triumph's integrated design, and in keeping with their principle of controlling all elements of the design, Triumph developed their own twin-barrel carburettor and a magneto system which they fitted for the 1908 season.

It was around this time that the Trusty Triumph nickname first appeared. Although belt drive was still used, Triumph also offered a new transmission system using a Sturmey-Archer three-speed rear hub similar to that used on pedal cycles. It was fitted with a clutch incorporated into the hub.

*Light in construction and weight  the 1913 3½hp model was reliable and easy to manage, later earning it the nickname 'Trusty Triumph'.*

*A simple side-valve design (above), the engine uses direct belt drive to the rear wheel. A hub gear and clutch made for a much easier life than the alternative fixed gear.*

More models joined the range, including the 225cc two-stroke 'Baby' and sporting variants aimed at the large number of riders who wanted to take part in motorcycle competitions. Triumph's own efforts had paid off with a win for Marshall in the second TT of 1908, and places in 1909 and 1910. Although Triumph machines failed to place in 1911, the marque's endurance had been proved by an epic Land's End to John O'Groats run undertaken by Ivan Hart-Davies, who rode 886 miles in just over 29 hours, the last time such a record run was permitted.

By 1911, the flagship of the range was the 3½hp model. Developed from the earlier 3hp machine, it carried many detail improvements, while the capacity had been increased by some 163cc. More new models followed, until the range embraced a direct belt-drive Roadster, a de-luxe version with a pedal-operated clutch, a sporting TT Roadster and a full TT racing model.

Such machines were capable of high sustained speeds – a TT racing Triumph could top 75mph – while Alfred Catt proved the 3½hp machines reliability with a phenomenal ride of over 2500 miles in six days, on roads that in the main were little better than cart tracks. His own health was permanently affected, but the Triumph earned a place in motorcycle history.

Another development would soon earn the company an even bigger place in history, with a larger 4hp (550cc) version called the Model H just before World War I. The motorcycle mainstay of the war effort, some 30,000 of Triumph's Model H were built, staying in use for many post-war years.

## Triumph 3½hp (1913)

*Years in production:* 1906–14
*Engine type:* single-cylinder
    side-valve four-stroke
*Bore and stroke:* 85 x 88mm
*Capacity:* 499cc,
*Carburettor:* Triumph twin-
    barrel
*Tyres (front/rear):* 2¼in x 26in
    / 2¼in x 26in
*Top speed:* approx 55mph

# Lea-Francis

At a time when all motorcycles were something of a luxury item the products of Lea-Francis were aimed at the top of the market. Concentrating on quality rather than quantity, they built on the solid reputation of Lea-Francis bicycles.

Bicycle manufacture had begun in 1895, when Graham Ingoldsby Francis and Richard Lea went into partnership in Coventry. Their 'safety bicycles' were built to the highest standards, and they had a smart showroom in Piccadilly, London.

Unlike many others, Lea-Francis dabbled in car manufacture before undertaking serious experiments

### Lea-Francis (1913–14)

*Years in production:* 1913–14
*Engine type:* JAP side-valve
  V-twin four-stroke
*Bore and stroke:* 85 x 88mm
*Capacity:* 430cc,
*Carburettor:* Amac
*Transmission:* all-chain with
  two-speed gearbox and
  multiplate clutch
*Top speed:* 55mph

*Rider conveniences abounded on the machines produced by Lea-Francis at their Coventry works The kickstart, footboards, enclosed chain drive and excellent weather protection were all rarities when the model was introduced, while the patented brakes were supposed to be the best or their kind.*

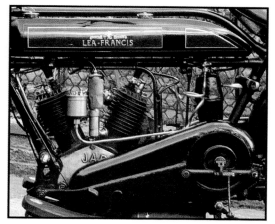

*The JAP V-twin (left) was a popular choice of many motorcycle manufacturers, with few weakness except for a tendency to overheat. Lea-Francis teamed it with their own two-speed gearbox, resulting in one of the best packages of the time.*

with motorcycles, although they did try fitting a proprietary engine to one of the bicycles in 1902. The Lea-Francis car appeared the following year, but it was never a commercial success.

The first motorcycle proper came out in 1912, with a 430cc JAP V-twin side-valve engine. It had a two-speed gearbox and a hefty price that emphasised its quality and concentration on providing the rider with the best of everything. This included excellent weather shielding, with large mudguards, footboards and full enclosure for the all-chain transmission. An under-tray swung forward to act as a stand, and the front brake used a dummy belt rim and friction block. The brakes, like the firm's reflex rear lamp, were under patent and said to be 'above suspicion'.

The chain drive and multiplate clutch were both advanced features for the time, when most makers relied on the simple belt. The method of tensioning the chain was also ingenious, for the gearbox was cylindrical, with an eccentric mounting. Simply rotating it in its housing provided a wide range of adjustment – a system that was seen almost 50 years later, when it was taken up for AJS and Matchless lightweights.

In 1914, Lea-Francis exhibited a range of new models with 430, 500 and 750cc JAP or MAG engines. However, the outbreak of war interrupted operations. A small number of machines were built for military use, but production virtually came to a halt. After the armistice, the V-twins returned much as before. The three-speed gearbox appeared in 1920, but by 1924 the company was concentrating on car production, so motorcycle manufacture was discontinued.

Gordon Francis had joined his father-in-law Arthur Barnett, in 1919, to form the Francis-Barnett partnership. The marque went on to build its own enviable reputation, including racing and off-road awards, and, as part of the AMC Group, survived until as late as 1964.

*A famous partnership: the Lea-Francis' tank badge (left) is flanked by the lever for the two-speed gear and the sight glass for the hand-pumped lubrication system.*

# Royal Enfield V-twin

Right from the beginning, Royal Enfield were proud to associate their motorcycles with their interests in small arms manufacture. 'Made like a gun' became a company slogan, and the pioneer machines gained an enviable reputation for reliability.

Longevity was another of the company's qualities, for having made their first machines in the early years of the century, they were one of the last to founder in the 1970s. The marque attained a kind of life after death, for Enfields are still made in Madras, India, to a design based on an original British pattern.

The first Royal Enfield was a quadricycle made in 1898, and together with tricycles that also used the ubiquitous De Dion engine, these comprised the bulk of the company's output for some years.

The Enfield Cycle Company started as a bicycle manufacturer in the 1890s but was absorbed by Eadie, which was in turn taken over by BSA in the early 1900s, at which point Royal Enfield went its own way. Though based in Redditch, Worcestershire, the firm was closely associated with the Royal Small Arms factory in Enfield, Middlesex, for which it made components. It was through this connection that the bike's name and badge, which depicted a rifle with fixed bayonet, originated.

## Royal Enfield V-twin (1914)

*Years in production:* 1913–20
*Engine type:* inlet-over-exhaust V-twin
  four-stroke
*Capacity:* 450cc
*Transmission:* chain, with cush-drive hub
*Top speed:* approx 65mph

*The V-twin Enfield became an enduring favourite, whether in solo or sidecar form. With the company's own design of transmission, most were powered by Swiss Motosaccoche engines, the London-built 6hp JAP being an exception.*

The first two-wheelers, which appeared in 1901, had a 211cc Minerva engine clamped to a bicycle frame, with twisted-belt drive to the rear wheel. One design had the engine in front of the steering head, another mounted on the front downtube. Both these options soon proved to be inferior to the Werner solution with the engine in the centre of the frame and this was rapidly adopted. An early Enfield idea that persisted through the company's life was the notion of carrying the lubricating oil in a chamber that was cast into the crankcase.

For the next few years, the firm dabbled in car manufacture, which meant that it was not until 1910 that real progress on the motorcycle front resulted. This time, the power unit was a 346cc V-twin designed by the Swiss company Motosaccoche. The new machines also included a two-speed gear using paired primary chains. Another innovation was the use of a rear hub with rubber inserts to provide a cush-drive. The firm expanded, starting to build its own engines, mostly V-twins of various sizes and regularly entered competitive events such the TT. However, production was cut short by the war. Their V-twin sidecar outfits were used by the military to great effect as machine-gun platforms, but only in limited numbers. But in the post-war era, the firm's fortunes rapidly revived with a light-weight two-stroke single that had been launched, but not fully exploited before the conflict began.

*The Enfield's V-twin engine (above) is an inlet-over-exhaust design, with the advanced feature of automatic lubrication via a double-acting pump.*

# Scott 3¾ Two Speed

One of the true pioneers, Alfred Angus Scott was an original thinker whose contributions to the fledgling motorcycle industry were many and various. Although Scott himself left the company he founded as early as 1919, the two-stroke machines built in the 1920s and 30s were some of the most charming motorcycles of the era, while Scott's ideas continued to influence successors as late as the 1970s Silk.

The list of Scott firsts and patents is extraordinary: including first rotary valves on a two-stroke, first telescopic forks, first kick-starter, one of the earliest parallel twins, and water-cooled motorcycle engines, and one of the first fully triangulated frames.

The man himself was born in 1874 in Bradford. Trained as an engineer, he worked for a time on marine steam engines, the layout of which had an influence on his designs. He began his own experiments early. In 1897, he patented a new type of bicycle brake, and around the end of the 19th century completed a twin-cylinder two-stroke engine, which he used to power the front wheel of his bicycle by friction drive to the tyre.

The experiments continued and the machine gained a transmission to the rear wheel. In 1904, Scott patented the engine design.

*Unconventional in almost every respect, but superbly logical, Scott's water-cooled two-speed twin-cylinder two-strokes won many competitions.*

## Scott 3¾ Two Speed (1913)

*Years in production:* 1908–26
*Engine type:* Parallel twin-cylinder water-cooled two-stroke
*Bore and stroke:* 73 x 63.5mm
*Capacity:* 532cc
*Carburation:* Scott carburettor
*Gearbox:* two-speed drive by chains with alternative ratio
*Wheelbase:* 55½in
*Weight:* 250lb

The first fully fledged Scott motorcycle was drawn up in 1908, and Scott contracted Jowett brothers, local engineers to manufacture the design for him. The 333cc air-cooled twin showed most features that would become Scott hallmarks. The frame was entirely made of straight tubes, and the revolutionary two-speed gear gave high or low ratios. In 1910, the machine was the first two-stroke to finish a TT, while in 1911 it set the record lap. In 1912, it led from start to finish, winning again in 1913.

Scott's civilian production continued until 1916, when his ideas found concrete expression with the design of a military three-wheeled gun carrier, and in 1919, he left the company to concentrate on the design of an unconventional three-wheeler called the 'Sociable', based on the gun-car. This never caught on and in 1923 Scott died after contracting pneumonia. He was only 48, and the company that he founded had many successful years to come.

# Clyno

Solid and well-engineered, the Clyno V-twin had reached its peak of development on the eve of World War I. Its qualities were not lost on the military authorities, who adopted the machine as the main standard issue for the Motor Machine Gun Service. Equipped with a sidecar platform and a heavy machine gun, and operating in threes, the machines provided a highly mobile attack force.

Clyno itself had begun manufacturing motorcycles only a few years earlier, but had been formed in 1908 as an accessory maker, in Thrapston, Northamptonshire. Founded by two cousins called Smith, the outfit's first product was a patented, adjustable inclined driving pulley, from which the firm took its name – a play on the word 'inclined'. The pulley was joined by a range of other useful accessories, and Clyno was soon profitable enough to go into motorcycle manufacture using proprietary V-twin and single-cylinder engines made by the Wolverhampton firm of Stevens, and fittings from Chater Lea in London.

*The massively engineered kick-start quadrant is typical of the Clyno's practical and robust construction.*

The new machines first appeared at the end of 1909 and were very successful, and a year later when there was a problem with the supply of engines, Clyno simply took over the engine manufacturer's works and machinery. Machines with Clyno's own engines began to appear from the Wolverhampton works at the end of 1910. The single-cylinder bike was dropped. The next year, a six-model range was on offer, all with the advanced feature of all-chain drive, a kickstart and even a two- or four-speed gearbox offering a choice of alternative chain ratios.

By 1913, the Clyno had become a byword for convenience, with such features as quickly detachable

wheels and cast-alloy footboards. With a neat and workman-like finish, it was robustly engineered, as befitted its favoured role as sidecar haulier. These qualities helped it to win favour at the military trials organised in 1914, and the substantial demand led to extra staff and long shifts to build the armoured combinations. From 1917, the Russian army was also supplied with a similar model.

Clyno might have been expected to profit from the post-war boom, but their chief designer left for rivals Raleigh, and their founder had turned his attention to the light car market. Ultimately, this situation spelt doom for the company, as it was unable to ride out the Depression.

## Clyno (1914)

*Engine type:* Side-valve V-twin four-stroke
*Capacity:* 744cc
*Carburettor:* Amac
*Transmission:* all-chain with three-speed countershaft gearbox and clutch
*Lubrication:* semi-automatic, with hand operated pump
*Top speed:* 55mph

*Handsome and sturdy, the Clyno typified the final development of the pre-World War I motorcycle as a practical comfortable solo or sidecar mount. It was these qualities that won it an important military contract, which saw it built in substantial numbers throughout the war years.*

# Douglas 2¾hp

Douglas flat-twin motorcycles won undying fame, and fortune, with their performance in World War 1, when the company equipped army despatch riders with some 25,000 machines. Technically advanced, they demonstrated the smoothness of an engine type that was adopted by numerous other manufacturers, and used by Douglas themselves as late as 1957.

The Douglas Engineering Company was founded in Bristol in 1882, by Scottish brothers William and Edward Douglas, as a general engineering company and foundry. But the Douglas motorcycle really grew out of the efforts of one Joseph Barter, who founded a company called Light Motors Ltd in nearby Kingswood. Barter had developed a design called the Fairy – which used a horizontally opposed engine of advanced design.

*Gear selection is controlled by the handle on top of the ·tank (left), which selects low or high ratio. Also visible is the hand pump used to supply oil to the engine.*

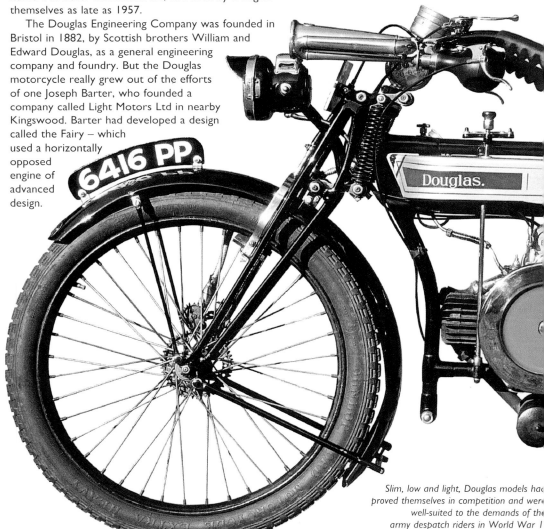

*Slim, low and light, Douglas models had proved themselves in competition and were well-suited to the demands of the army despatch riders in World War 1*

Despite its technical advantages, Barter failed to make enough money to enable the firm to survive, and in 1907, Douglas took over manufacture of a model based on the Fairy, enlarging the engine size to 2¾hp (340cc). In 1910, a new two-speed gearbox was fitted under the gearbox and operated by a handle on top of the tank. Belt drive was used and no clutch was fitted. The new model won an important reliability trial, and set a record for the Lands End to John O'Groats run. In 1912, the engine gained new, mechanically operated valves that gave a power output of some 8bhp. At that year's Isle of Man TT, there were several Douglas entries which gained outstanding successes. By the end of 1914, Douglas had sold around 12,000 machines and they soon became one of the most important makers of military machines.

For a small side-valve, the Douglas twin was quick, and being light, it was easy to manhandle. The front plug could short out in the wet, but on the whole the machine was very reliable and smooth running. After the war, a civilian version of the Douglas twin went back into production in 1919, but many ex-WD examples were reconditioned and sold off, giving long and honourable service in peace just as they had in war-time.

## Douglas 2¾hp (1919)

*Years in production:* 1912–22
*Engine type:* horizontally opposed side-valve four-stroke twin
*Bore and stroke:* 60.8 x 60mm
*Capacity:* 348cc
*Power:* 8bhp
*Carburettor:* Douglas two-lever
*Tyres (front/rear):* 2¼in x 26in/ 2¼in x 26in
*Weight:* 170lb
*Top speed:* 40mph

# Wooler

Despite its late date of manufacture, Wooler's unorthodox twin is a true pioneer in spirit. A tiny maker, led by a true visionary who seemed to delight in the unusual, the company survived until the 1950s, albeit with a gap of 17 years. Unusual engine configurations and suspension designs were a Wooler hallmark, as was the styling which was cleverly designed to turn heads.

John Wooler built his first motorcycle in 1911, and it set the pattern for the future. The engine was a horizontal single-cylinder two-stroke with a double-ended piston, eliminating the need for normal crankcase compression. The power was transmitted by a long pin that stuck through slots in the crankcase walls with external connecting rods to the flywheel. A front and rear suspension, way ahead of its time, used a patented plunger system. The patent also covered a fuel tank that enclosed the steering head, supposedly as a means of achieving greater fuel capacity.

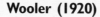

That first machine had a 230cc engine, but by the time it went into production the engine had been enlarged to 344cc. There were many minor improvements, including knock-through wheel spindles and nuts of only two sizes. That led to a trade-mark of a double-ended spanner and the word 'Accessibility'. The Wilkinson Wooler was in production until 1913, and manufacture ceased during World War I.

> ## Wooler (1920)
>
> *Years in production:* 1919-23
> *Engine type:* horizontally opposed (fore-and-aft) inlet-over-exhaust four-stroke
> *Bore and stroke:* 60 x 60mm
> *Capacity:* 348cc
> *Transmission:* initially by variable ratio belt, later by chain drive
> *Weight:* 162lb
> *Top speed:* 55mph

The Wooler that appeared in 1919 was similar in layout but very different in almost every detail of the engine. This was now a 350cc four-stroke flat-twin, similar to the popular Douglas, but of inlet-over-exhaust layout rather than a side-valve. The forward-projecting tank was completely redesigned, but the suspension and variable belt-drive systems were there as before.

A real lightweight, the Wooler was also astoundingly economical. During a special test, it achieved an amazing 311 miles to the gallon. At Brooklands, it broke 29 world long-distance endurance records. and gained its 'Flying Banana' nickname.

After 1923, Wooler fitted new semi-overhead-cam 350 and 500cc versions of the engine. In 1926, he tried a much more conventional machine with rigid frame and fairly conventional girder forks with a 511cc single-cylinder engine. Wooler's small factory in Wembley produced a small range of motorcycles until 1930, when it closed down.

In 1936, Wooler had begun work on another incredibly unconventional design. A 500cc trans-verse four with pistons interconnected by rocking beams to a single big end. Sadly, this incredibly lightweight design did not proceed beyond the early experimental stage.

*The horizontally-opposed engine (below) was extremely efficient, covering 311 miles on a gallon of fuel in a special test.*

*The nickname 'Flying Banana' came from the size, shape and colour of its tank. Despite its unconventional appearance, the Wooler won 29 world records for speed and endurance.*

Manufacturers' badges 1900–1919

# VINTAGE DAYS

## —— 1920–1940 ——

ABC ✪ Levis Popular ✪ Norton 16H
Velocette Two-stroke ✪ Triumph Ricardo
BSA Round Tank ✪ James V-twin ✪ Brough Superior
Ner-a-car ✪ Cotton TT ✪ Sunbeam Model 90
Velocette KTT ✪ Norton CS1 ✪ Scott Squirrel
Matchless Silver Hawk ✪ Excelsior Manxman
Norton International ✪ Vincent Rapide ✪
Triumph Speed Twin 5T ✪ BSA Gold Star
✪ Rudge Ulster

# Vintage Days

Although World War I ended in November 1918, rationing remained in force for some time and it was not until the following year that motorcycle factories were allowed to go back into production.

However, the end of the war coincided with an enormous demand for transport, fuelled by the returning servicemen and women, many of whom had their first experience of motorcycles or cars while at arms.

At first this demand was met by secondhand pre-war models or reconditioned military machines, of which there were many thousands – mostly the ubiquitous despatch riders' Triumph single or Douglas twin. Prices were high, there were long waiting lists and fuel was in short supply, but demand was steady. The situation was tailor-made for ingenious dealers and accessory manufacturers to offer ways to make an old model appear like a new one, or economise with gadgets such as fuel-savers, 'hot' exhausts and plug protectors.

When restrictions on manufacture were lifted, there still remained the problem of limited raw materials, including most metals and rubber. Manufacturing capacity was no problem at all; there was a host of factories that had been forced to turn their attention from profitable and intensive war work to the civilian market. For firms such as

*Typical of a host of small factories in the immediate post-war years, Sheffield-Henderson was a sidecar maker that assembled machines around proprietary engines from Blackburne.*

Triumph, it was simply a matter of reopening the production lines, but there were others with no pre-war experience, for whom the seller's market was impossible to resist. Factories that had until recently been building aircraft, tanks or munitions began to turn their attention to motorcycles.

By the end of 1919, there were at least 50 new manufacturers and within two years this had risen to over a hundred. More than two hundred models were exhibited at the first post-war Olympia show in 1919. Some of these were gimcrack designs, hastily rushed into production, others were simply 'assembly jobs' relying on bought-in engines.

*Railway and shipbuilding conglomerates such as Beardmore got in on the act. This is a 1921 350cc Beardmore-Precision.*

*Working bikes (right): motoring organisations were quick to catch on to the practicality of the motorcycle. In 1922, these four RAC patrolmen were equipped with Ivy 250cc two-strokes.*

*Motorcycles were a staple form of transport in the inter-war years. Lightweights, such as the 225cc Royal Enfield shown below, were favoured by the taxation laws.*

For the most part there was little immediate technical advancement, for the war had shown what was worthwhile. The emphasis tended to be on reliability and convention. BSA, Matchless, Sunbeam and Clyno all showed machines that would have seemed familiar six years earlier. Others such as Royal Enfield were prepared to experiment, with their prototype four-cylinder machine, which failed to go into production. But the star of the show was the revolutionary ABC, manufactured by the Sopwith Aviation company. Representing a huge technological leap, this above all seemed to presage a new direction for the industry, although the detail flaws and financial muddle that attended its launch were indicative of the age in a less attractive way. Other industrial giants were not far behind, such as Beardmore with their Precision design that again proved to promise more than it delivered.

Production got into full swing in 1920, but the euphoric promises of a year before all too often proved impossible to keep. Many prices were much higher than had been suggested.

Competitions had also returned in 1919. Hill-climbs, sprints and trials regained all their pre-war popularity, while the Isle of Man TT and Brooklands were back in 1920. An ABC won at the first Brooklands event while Sunbeam, AJS and Levis took the TTs. The 1920s ushered in what many call the 'Golden Age' of motorcycling. According to the strict definition, a 'Vintage' bike is deemed to be one constructed before 1930.

As prosperity returned, customers increased in numbers and the successful factories boomed. Motorcycling was seen as socially acceptable for all classes. A motorcycle could provide a family with transport or be a workaday tool. Sidecars were built with enough seats for a large family, or designed for butchers and bakers to transport their wares. A solo motorcycle was a very fashionable accessory for the young who could afford the latest 'race replica'.

The basic motorcycle was similar to its pre-war counterpart – usually a 500cc single cylinder side-valve – made by Triumph or Norton. There was also a boom in lightweights, such as the Levis and Royal Enfield, partly as a result of a 1921 regulation which halved the tax payable if the machine was under 200lb in weight. This helped the motorcycle appeal to a whole new breed of rider.

*Family transport (above): throughout the 1920s motorcycles and sidecar outfits were an eminently respectable means of travelling, and sales boomed.*

Speeds also began to rise and sports machines grew in popularity. In 1924, a Blackburne-engined Chater-Lea became the first 350cc to exceed 100mph at Brooklands. Much of the interest in motorcycling was fuelled by the glamour of racing, and in particular the TT, which attracted huge crowds throughout the period. Stars such as Stanley Woods, Jimmy Simpson and Wal Handley were household names, while riders such as Bert Le Vack and Freddie Dixon became famous for their record-breaking exploits, hoisting the world record to almost 130 mph by the end of the decade. Norton and Velocette, among other manufacturers, built their reputations with a string of wins that proved Britain really did build the best bikes in the world. Such new sports as dirt-track (speedway) sprang up and proved hugely popular with the crowds.

It was only at the end of the 1920s that light cars such as the Morris Minor and Austin Seven began to

*The Isle of Man TT : a famous incident in 1924 (above) as Stanley Woods corners his Cotton ahead of Norton's Joe Craig, who has fallen at Governor's Bridge. Woods became the most successful rider of his generation while Craig went on to become head of Norton's race shop in their glory days.*

*Pressed-steel and a Villiers engine were Francis-Barnett's solution to providing low-budget transport. The 1937 Cruiser model offered comfort and cleanliness and was a popular 30s alternative.*

offer a challenge to the motorcycle. There were three-quarters of a million bikes – a third of the world's total – on Britain's roads in 1929, when the New York stock exchange collapsed. The shock waves of the Depression soon reached Britain.

That year's motor show had seen the buoyant launch of new luxury models, but economy would soon become the byword. Weaker manufacturers went to the wall, while others turned to new ideas such as hire purchase. Prices went down and then reached rock bottom in 1932, when the annual show at Olympia was cancelled. A year later the taxation classes were revised to favour smaller machines. By 1936, the 250cc pushrod-engined Red Panther offered well over 110 mpg and cost less than £30 cash, payable in weekly instalments of some 33p. Motorcycle sport continued to prosper, perhaps as an antidote to the drab austerity of the times. But commercially things failed to improve and many famous factories were forced to close or merge – Ariel, the second largest concern in the land, AJS, Douglas and Sunbeam among them. One of the most significant factors in the shape of the postwar industry was also taking place in the Midlands, where Edward Turner, late of Ariel, now of Triumph, was laying down the form of the Speed Twin, a model that would dictate the form of the motorcycle for three decades and more.

*BSA, for a time the biggest manufacturer in the world, got big by making good honest workhorses like the 1934 'Sloper'.*

Meanwhile, an increasing continental challenge to British sporting supremacy was being mounted by Italian and German motorcycles. The great Stanley Woods switched to Moto Guzzi in 1935 and won two TTs for the Italian team and BMW, NSU and DKW began fielding technically advanced racers trying to demonstrate Germany's engineering supremacy. By the end of the 1930s, however, British industry was gearing up for a greater conflict on a wider front. Within months Europe was at war, drawing another chapter in motorcycle history to a close.

*Norton and Velocexe were a British racing double-act throughout the 1920s and 30s. Norton star P (Tim) Hunt pushes off in the 1932 Junior.*

# ABC

In 1919, many manufacturers who had been involved in war work found themselves facing the prospect of cutting back their activities unless they could diversify into other types of production. One such was Sopwith of Kingston-on-Thames, Surrey, an aircraft company that faced a sudden downturn in demand. Proprietor Tommy Sopwith believed that motorcycle production could be the answer, and turned to the designer Granville Bradshaw for help.

The solution that Bradshaw offered was the astonishingly bold ABC flat-twin – even more extraordinary because the design was completed in a mere 11 days. He had bet Sopwith that a prototype could be produced in three weeks – and backed this claim with a deal

whereby he staked £100 per day over that time, while Sopwith would pay a similar sum for every day less. As a result, Bradshaw netted £1000 on the deal.

A machine built so quickly might have been expected to be crude, or at the least a copy of an existing design, but the ABC was neither. Its horizontally-opposed twin-cylinder engine employed overhead-valves and it had an integral four-speed gearbox.

When it was launched, the ABC captured the imagination of the reviewers. Light weight and quiet, the machine had a brisk performance, as well as being comfortable and stable. Orders began to flood in and the French company Gnôme et Rhône were signed up to produce the design under licence.

*The valve gear (left), in its original form proved too weak. The firm's financial difficulties meant that they were never really able to develop the ABC fully.*

Rider comfort was a key part of the ABC concept. Front and rear springing, wide footboards and legshields offered a relaxed ride, with sophisticated controls.

## ABC (1919)

Years in production: 1919–25
Engine type: horizontally
    opposed twin-cylinder
    overhead-valve four-stroke
Bore and stroke: 68.6 x 54mm
Capacity: 398cc
Carburettor: Claudel-Hobson
Gearbox: four-speed with
    H-gate
Top speed: 70mph

Rider convenience: the four-speed gearbox (below) was innovative, and the carburettor was simpler to control than most contemporaries.

Then the troubles began. Initially priced at £70, the ABC proved too expensive to manufacture, and the design had to be modified to sort out some mechanical problems. Sales should have begun early in 1919, but when the first machines appeared in May 1920, the price had risen to an astronomical £160, and even at this price the makers were hardly covering their costs.

Only some 2000 were made. Although the ABCs proved capable of winning two speed records in the year they were launched, it soon transpired that the valve gear was weak and prone to breakage. While accessory makers offered cures for its mechanical problems, the factory itself quietly let the unprofitable ABC fade away. The last one made by Sopwith was built in 1923, although Gnôme et Rhône made a few up until 1925. After that it was left to others – especially the flat-twin BMWs – to demonstrate what the concept might have offered.

# Levis Popular

Simple and cheap, Levis' lightweight was typical of the machines that provided everyday transport for the masses in the years just after World War I. But with its quality of engineering, it was also perhaps the best of its kind, and the name Levis went on to become a byword for two-stroke machines that were reliable, light and quick.

Levis motorcycles were made by Butterfields Ltd, a Birmingham engineering firm started in 1906 by two brothers, William and Arthur Butterfield. In 1910, they successfully tested their own two-stroke engine and produced their first machine which was only a little more substantial than a bicycle. With its 196cc two-stroke engine and direct belt drive to the rear wheel, it was capable of some 35mph. For their slogan, Butterfields adopted the Latin phrase *levis et celer* meaning 'light and fast', and took the name Levis for the name of the motorcycles.

When the machine went into production as the Levis Model 1, the engine size had been increased to 269cc, there was also a 211cc version, the Baby Levis. In the years before World War I, Butterfields went on to offer a number of versions of these models, together with a 349cc De-Luxe. In 1914, the 211cc Popular was introduced, along with a 175cc Levisette.

The war, of course, put paid to much further development, although the firm experimented with engines for the aircraft industry. But in the years immediately after peace returned, there was an urgent need for cheap transport, which Levis stepped in to fill.

Levis had also begun racing, and in 1920 entered 250cc machines in the Junior (350cc) TT, which included a newly introduced trophy for machines of 250cc or less in which they took first, second, and third.

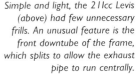

*Simple and light, the 211cc Levis (above) had few unnecessary frills. An unusual feature is the front downtube of the frame, which splits to allow the exhaust pipe to run centrally.*

*Very unusually for a simple two-stroke of the time, the carburettor (left) supplies only a petrol/air mixture. Oil is provided from a separate reservoir, which feeds directly to the bottom end of the engine.*

## Levis Popular (1921)

*Years in production:* 1914–24
*Engine type:* single-cylinder
   two-stroke with drip feed
   lubrication
*Bore and stroke:* 62 x 70mm
*Capacity:* 211cc
*Carburettor:* Amac
*Tyres (front/rear):* 2¼in x 24in/
   2¼in x 24in
*Weight:* 118lb
*Fuel consumption:* 150mpg
*Top speed:* 35mph

Among the machines that provided Levis' bread and butter, the Popular was perhaps the most important. It had a simple construction, with a light frame and forks and a transmission consisting of a belt looped around the engine pulley, driving the back wheel. With no kick-start or gears, starting was by pushing off, using a decompression lever to help the engine turn over easily. A large external flywheel kept the engine running evenly, although it might slow to a fast walking pace when pulling uphill. Brakes were simple, too, with a bicycle-type stirrup brake on the front rim and a heel-operated rear brake.

But such simplicity did not mean crudeness. The Levis was well-engineered and simple to repair. It even included such sophistication as separate oiling, at a time when most two-strokes relied on a premixed petrol. It was a formula that kept it in production until 1924 – a run of over a decade – when more apparently sophisticated models from both Levis and their rivals had come and gone.

# Norton 16H

Tracing its lineage back to 1911, the Norton 16H was by turns a TT racer, wartime despatch machine and family sidecar slogger, in a remarkable career that spanned 33 years. In all that time, the engine's basic layout remained unchanged – it was simply that the world moved on around it.

In 1911, the Isle of Man TT included a 500cc Senior class for the first time, and Norton had a new design ready to contest it. A side-valve of 490cc with dimensions of 79 x 100mm bore and stroke, it was listed as the '3½'. Founder James Norton rode one of the firm's entries himself, but failed to place. Yet, the very next year, a similar machine won the Brooklands TT, and three world records in the one event. In 1913, versions on sale included the Brooklands Special (BS) and Brooklands Road Special (BRS), which with their single-speed belt-driven transmission were guaranteed to have lapped Brooklands at more than 70mph (65 for the BRS), while many were in fact capable of exceeding 80mph.

| Norton 16H (1922) | |
|---|---|
| *Years in production:* | 1921–54 |
| *Engine type:* | single-cylinder side-valve four-stroke |
| *Bore and stroke:* | 79 x 100mm |
| *Capacity:* | 490cc |
| *Compression ratio:* | 4.9:1 |
| *Power:* | 12bhp |
| *Tyres (front/rear):* | 3¼ x 26in |
| *Top speed:* | 78mph |

*Sporting sidecar (right): the 16H was often linked to a sidecar throughout its long production life, although by the end it was providing family transport rather than race entries.*

*Lean and low-slung, the 1922 Norton 16H helped to establish a style for fast sporting 'flat-tankers'.*

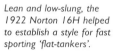

A chain-driven version was developed, but with World War I intervening it was 1919 before the 490cc Norton was back in civilian production. The catalogued Model 16 now featured chain-drive with a three-speed Sturmey-Archer gearbox, and was directly related to the competition machines that were holders of some 21 world records. In 1920, at the first post-war TT, half the finishers were riding Nortons.

The next year, Norton launched a new model, called the Colonial. Aimed at the expanding market in less developed areas of the Empire, it had a higher ground clearance than the standard machine, which gained an even lower riding position and a new designation – the 16H ('H' for Home) model.

In 1922, Norton's race development effort switched to the newly designed overhead-valve Model 18. Out of the spotlight, the 16H found a new role as a popular sporting tourer. The engine was reworked in 1931, but the next major change came in 1936, when after earlier successful trials the army began to place regular orders for 16Hs (modified for off-road work). Continued right through the war, more than 80,000 were delivered, spanning a decade in all. Some machines stayed in service until the late 1950s.

# Velocette Two-stroke

*Slim, low and light with a sophisticated engine, the Velocette two-stroke won many admirers, and gave its name to 60 years of successors.*

The British manufacturing company Veloce was founded in 1905 by John Gutgemann, a German who later anglicised his name to Goodman. Veloce was a family concern which made a wide range of products, including bicycles and conventional 500cc motorcycles. When they decided to add a speedy lightweight two-stroke to the line-up, the name Velocette was chosen to suggest that it was a baby version of the bigger machines. In time the new baby became so popular that the company was named after it rather than the other way around.

Although beautifully engineered and light, the frame and forks were conventional, and the real interest lay in the engine and transmission. These were both very sophisticated for their day, and offered many advanced features.

The transmission was by chain throughout - at a time when many competitors relied on the much less reliable belt. It had the luxury of a two-speed gearbox, although no clutch was fitted. The gearchange was by a large knob, fitted on the right of the tank.

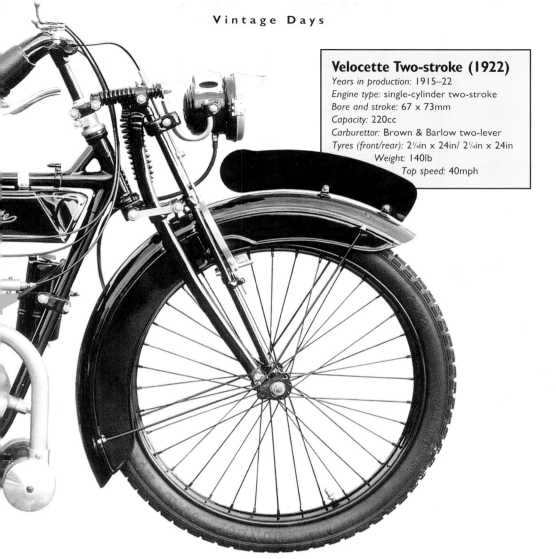

**Velocette Two-stroke (1922)**
*Years in production:* 1915–22
*Engine type:* single-cylinder two-stroke
*Bore and stroke:* 67 x 73mm
*Capacity:* 220cc
*Carburettor:* Brown & Barlow two-lever
*Tyres (front/rear):* 2¼in x 24in/ 2¼in x 24in
*Weight:* 140lb
*Top speed:* 40mph

Part of the reason for the absence of a clutch was the crankcase design, which was very compact and very narrow, giving a very stiff bottom end. On the early two-stroke, only one main bearing was used, and the crank was overhung. To balance it, the flywheel was fitted externally, and the drive chain ran inside this. The benefit of the crankcase design was its strength, with a lubrication system that offered reliable oiling under all conditions. Most two-strokes then and for the next 50 years relied on hit-and-miss oiling by petrol lubrication.

The top end was conventional for a two-stroke of the period, using a side-mounted induction tract and deflector type piston to control the gas flow. Because of the absence of a clutch, a compression relief valve was fitted to the front of the cylinder head to allow the engine to spin easily when starting off. In use the little Velocette was reliable and economical, while the absence of a clutch was no hardship at a time before heavy traffic existed. Simple and well-engineered, it paved the way for the company's success during the 1920s and 30s.

# Triumph Ricardo

Having established an enviable reputation in the early days of motorcycle competition, Triumph chose to ignore events such as the Isle of Man TT for several years. So when they performed an abrupt about turn in 1922 it could be expected that they were pretty confident of the machine that they chose to enter – the super sports 'Ricardo'.

Sir Henry (Harry) Ricardo was a renowned combustion expert who had worked on behalf of many companies when he was asked by Triumph to advise on a replacement for their trusty side-valves. Ricardo produced a number of alternatives before Triumph announced that their new overhead-valve model would use a four-valve head design. In fact, from the cylinder barrel down, the rest of the machine was virtually identical to Triumph's tried-and-tested Model H side-valve.

The theoretical advantages of a four-valve head were numerous. Gas flow could be more efficient, the spark plug could be positioned centrally for more efficient combustion, and lighter components would respond quicker, allowing higher revs. In fact, Ricardo's design was quite conservative, using small ports and unusually recessed valves. Each pair of valves was parallel, set at 90 degrees to each other, with stems and springs exposed; the piston, which was of light alloy, had a concave crown and a slipper-type skirt. The cylinder barrel was made of solid steel and had deep finning, while the head, which had two parallel exhaust ports, was iron.

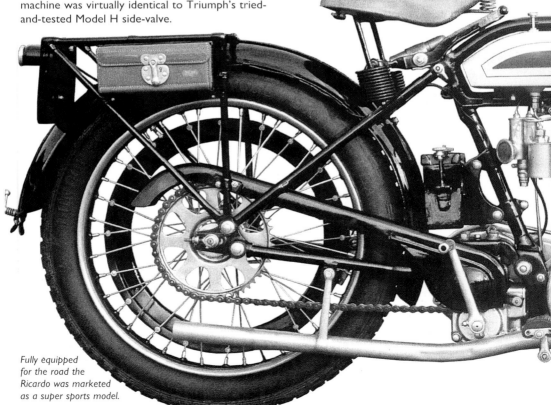

*Fully equipped for the road the Ricardo was marketed as a super sports model.*

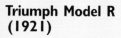

## Triumph Model R (1921)

*Years in production:* 1921–28
*Engine type:* single-cylinder
  four-valve ohv four-stroke
*Bore and stroke:* 80.5 x 98mm
*Capacity:* 499cc
*Power:* 20bhp @ 4600rpm
*Carburettor:* Triumph twin barrel
*Tyres (front/rear):* 3 x 26in/3 x 26in
*Transmission:* Triumph three-
  speed gearbox
*Weight:* 250lb
*Top speed:* 70mph

From there down, the engine was based on the Model H. The fly-wheels were slightly smaller, to allow free revving, while lubrication, relying on constant-loss fed by hand pump, was later changed to dry sump fed by external oil pump. The resulting Model R Fast Roadster was marketed as a fully equipped sports model and attracted favourable reports. In this form it lapped Brooklands at 68mph, while a racing version also took the hour record at almost 77mph, and a flying mile at nearly 84mph.

Three were entered for the 1921 TT, but handling deficiencies meant that only one finished. A year later, the Ricardo was back with the new lubrication system, stronger valve gear, a modi-fied cylinder with new dimensions and made of cast iron, a three-speed gearbox and new front fork. This time, it finished second in the TT, and the following year went on to take a number of continental wins and gold medals in the ISDT.

After 1924, Triumph switched their development efforts to a new model, although the 'Riccy' stayed in their range as a sports model until 1928. But the four-valve layout had proved its potential for the future.

# BSA Round Tank

For a long period in the inter-war years the giant BSA conglomerate dominated a booming motorcycle market in a way that no other British factory could claim to have done. 'One in four is a BSA' was a factory advertising slogan, and it was no idle boast. Part of the reason why BSA became so big was that they understood the needs of the market. While their machines were not the most glamorous – and for many years didn't race – they satisfied the demand for reliable transport that even underpins today's machines from the Japanese giants.

At one end of the market this meant heavy-weight sloggers such as the BSA V-twins and 500cc singles, often with sidecars as family transport or workaday hacks. At the other end of the market it meant affordable lightweights and, in particular, 250cc singles. Their attack on this market began in 1924 and was very much a new departure for BSA. It was known to be a difficult market, because over the preceding years, the public had been treated to many poorly designed and underengineered budget specials from other makers.

*The little BSA Round Tank was a well-loved utility machine that established its makers in this important market. Reliable and rugged, it put thousands of people on wheels.*

As a result, the little BSA was solidly conventional, with a side-valve four-stroke engine in place of the often unreliable two-stroke. It was strong enough to take all that the most uncaring rider could throw at it, and it was cheap – less than £40. There was belt-and-braces lubrication, with a new-fangled mechanical pump as well as the old-fashioned hand pump, plus a sight feed to reassure the anxious owner that all was well. The oil was contained in the front section of the cylindrical tank that gave the model its name. The mudguards were surely some of the widest ever fitted to a motorcycle, capable of guarding against any conditions. Indeed,

they were so wide that the front forks actually passed through them. All-chain drive was used, while the gearbox was operated directly by a long hand lever.

With such a concern for practicality it might seem odd that the factory chose not to fit a front brake. It was felt that, with a modest top speed, a back brake should be perfectly adequate. In fact, BSA's design coincided with the introduction of a new legal requirement that all machines should be fitted with two independent means of stopping. The factory solved that simply by fitting, in addition to the footbrake, a friction block operated by a handlebar lever that pressed on the dummy belt rim on the rear wheel.

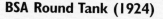

**BSA Round Tank (1924)**

*Years in production:* 1924–27
*Engine type:* single-cylinder side-valve
  four-stroke
*Capacity:* 249cc
*Bore and stroke:* 63 × 80mm
*Tyres:* 2¼ × 24in beaded-edge type
*Brakes:* friction block on dummy belt rim
  (rear only – two independent systems)
*Gearbox:* two-speed
*Top speed:* 43mph

The resulting machine was a pleasant utility bike that did a great deal to establish BSA's reputation for quality and reliability. One was even used as part of a BSA publicity stunt, in May 1924, to climb Mount Snowdon in Wales in just over half an hour, alongside the mountain railway track. The stunt was such a success that the motorcycle sold in large numbers – some 35,000 – and was adopted by the Post Office for telegram delivery. This remained a familiar role for BSA lightweights for many years, right up to the era of the BSA Bantam and the twilight of a once-great British company.

*Suspended between the frame rails on two nickel-plated suspension bands, the tank that gave the model its name had a separate oil compartment in front of the main petrol tank. Rather unkindly, the machine was also dubbed the 'Flying Marrow'.*

# James V-twin

In their later years, when they were simply part of the giant AMC group, the name of James would come to be associated almost exclusively with the kind of budget two-strokes that represented the final fling of the British industry. But in the early days, the picture was very different, and the marque adopted the slogan 'The Famous James' for its twin-cylinder flagship.

The company had been founded in the1870s as a bicycle manufacturer, taking the name of founder Harold James. The James Cycle Company, based in Greet, Birmingham, soon grew into a substantial operation. It produced its first motorcycle in 1902 which was virtually a conventional pedal cycle modified to take an engine, with belt drive to the rear wheel.

The earliest James machines used proprietary engines, but within a few years the company was manufacturing its own two-stroke and four-stroke power units, as well as experimenting with ideas such as drum brakes and quick-change wheels. The 1908 'Safety' model was influential on rival makers, and in 1911, James introduced a model with features such as multi-plate clutch, a kick-start, two-speed gearbox and all-chain drive.

During World War 1, James machines were used by the Allied forces, but a fire at the factory prevented them from going back into peacetime production immediately. The earliest post-war models produced were 250 and 350cc side-valve singles, and these were soon followed by popular V-twins of 500cc.

Popular as they were, the bigger James models were expensive to buy. By the end of the 1920s, the Depression was starting to bite and James were able to buy up the ailing Baker company, makers of lightweight motorcycles. From about 1930, smaller machines powered by proprietary Villiers two-strokes became the mainstay of James' business, until they themselves were taken over after World War 2.

The gearchange quadrant on the side of the tank (left) is a special alloy casting made in James' own foundry.

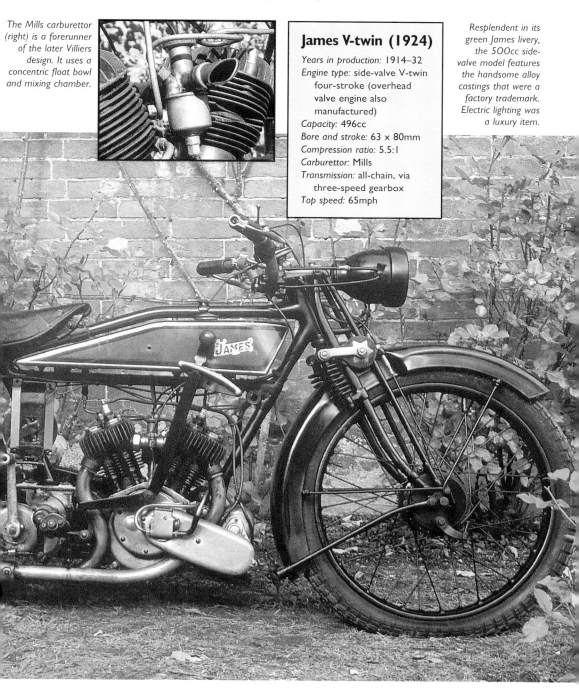

The Mills carburettor (right) is a forerunner of the later Villiers design. It uses a concentric float bowl and mixing chamber.

## James V-twin (1924)

*Years in production:* 1914–32
*Engine type:* side-valve V-twin four-stroke (overhead valve engine also manufactured)
*Capacity:* 496cc
*Bore and stroke:* 63 x 80mm
*Compression ratio:* 5.5:1
*Carburettor:* Mills
*Transmission:* all-chain, via three-speed gearbox
*Top speed:* 65mph

Resplendent in its green James livery, the 500cc side-valve model features the handsome alloy castings that were a factory trademark. Electric lighting was a luxury item.

# Brough Superior SS100

The Brough Superior has been called the first superbike. The aim of its designer George Brough was to build a machine that was 'the best'– and in its day the Brough Superior earned itself the title of the 'Rolls Royce of Motor Cycles'. The SS100 could top 100mph when half that speed was considered good going, looked like it cost a fortune – and did – and was the natural choice of the rich and famous.

George Brough's father William was a well-established motorcycle manufacturer who had built a range of machines at his Nottingham factory since the 1890s. But George, an excellent competition rider, wanted something with more performance than the Brough product could offer. So in 1919, after failing to convince his father of his ideas, George set up his own works in Nottingham.

In fact, almost every part of the Brough Superior was the product of another factory; engines mostly from the JAP factory in Tottenham, London, gearboxes by Sturmey-Archer, brakes from Enfield and so on. The forks were Harley-Davidson, later copied by Brough under their own 'Castle' trademark. But George Brough had chosen the best components available and put them together with a keen stylist's eye, to create something with a visual appeal that no other machine could better – and a performance to match. The earliest Brough Superiors had side-valve V-twin engines but were no slouches – 80mph being well within reach. The finish, with acres of nickel plate and enamel, was superb, and the tank, a Brough's crowning glory, was like no other.

## Brough Superior SS100 (1913)

Years in production: 1924–39
Engine type: 45° V-twin ohv four-stroke
Bore and stroke: 85.5 x 86mm
Capacity: 998cc
Carburettors: Binks
Tyres (front/rear): 3 x 28in/3 x 28in
Weight: 330lb
Top speed: 100mph

The distinctive, Brough tank (right) carries filler caps for oil and petrol and a sight-gauge for the oil feed, as well as a handsome chronometric speedometer.

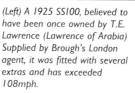

(Left) A 1925 SS100, believed to have been once owned by T.E. Lawrence (Lawrence of Arabia) Supplied by Brough's London agent, it was fitted with several extras and has exceeded 108mph.

The Brough name on the magneto drive (above) only told part of the story, for the V-twin engine was the product of the JAP factory in Tottenham, as attested by the crankcase casting.

George Brough was an excellent publicist, selling the machines with his own exploits. In 1922, he rode his personal Brough Superior SS80, nicknamed 'Spit and Polish' to win a Brooklands race at over 100mph, and took over 200 awards for his riding in trials and races. In 1922–3 he won 51 out of 52 sprints he entered.

In 1924, the first SS100 appeared. It had a 1000cc overhead-valve JAP V-twin engine and was based on the model on which rider Bert le Vack had taken the world speed record to 119mph. When launched, an SS100 cost between £150 and £170, according to specification – a huge sum when a modest house might cost £300 – but every model was guaranteed to have been tested at over 100mph and had handling to match. To add to the rider's comfort, the handlebars were made to suit the original owner. Acetylene gas lights were the standard fitting, although later bikes came with electric lights.

Those who could afford it, loved the Brough SS100 and it continued to be produced in small quantities, as befitted its high-quality status. In 1928, a long-stroke engine was introduced, which offered more power at the price of some flexibility. The JAP engine was redesigned in 1933, and in 1935 a Matchless engine was introduced. But in 1940, after two decades at the top, the Brough factory turned its production over to the war effort. When peace returned a period of post-war austerity followed, and with no suitable engines being made, it was to be the end of Brough motorcycles.

# Ner-a-car

The Ner-a-car was one of the most innovative 'motorcycles' ever made. A complete concept, it owed little to convention when it was designed, and embodied ideas that are still considered radical today. This makes it even more remarkable that in its day it was commercially successful enough to remain in production for some five years and sell in reasonable numbers.

Ner-a-car took its name from a double pun. Not only was it 'near a car' in its design principle, it was also the brainchild of an American called Carl Neracher. Working in a factory in Syracuse, New York State, Neracher built his first models in 1921, with the idea of making a machine that was more stable and comfortable than a conventional motorcycle could ever be. The basis of the design was a low-slung platform of pressed steel, which housed the engine, transmission and rear wheel.

Initially, there was no rear suspension, although this was later added. At the front, the frame splayed out to house the front wheel, which was suspended on coil springs with king-pin similar to a car's.

This form of hub-centre steering helped to make it possible for the machine to have an ultra-low centre of gravity and a more inherently precise control of steering and suspension. Its attraction is such that a similar principle has surfaced from time to time throughout motorcycle history, including on top of the range models from Yamaha and Bimota. Its chief drawback is the limited steering lock; in the case of the Ner-a-car leading to a turning circle of nearly 20 ft (over 6m).

This was a small price to pay for the machine's uncanny stability such that it could easily be ridden hands-off while with the huge front mudguard and wide footboards it offered excellent weather protection. The engine was under a cowling, which also helped to keep the rider clean. A later de-luxe model offered a windshield and instrument panel to give shielding as good as the best modern fairings.

At first, the power unit was a 211cc two-stroke single, and in this form the model was launched in Britain at the 1921 TT. The engine drove a large external flywheel, which also provided the transmission. The makers licensed the design to the British company Sheffield Simplex, who uprated the machine to 350cc side-valve and pushrod engines from proprietary makers Blackburne, together with a standard three-speed gearbox. The price of what had been an expensive machine came down and won many more customers. By 1926, Sheffield-Simplex was catering to their needs with the deluxe model's car-type seat and dashboard. Sadly, the market remained a limited one, and at the end of the year, production ceased for good.

## Ner-a-car (1925)

*Years in production:* 1921-26
*Engine type:* single-cylinder side-valve four-stroke
*Capacity:* 350cc
*Gearbox:* Sturmey-Archer three-speed
*Wheelbase:* 59in
*Turning circle:* 19ft 6in
*Weight:* 168lb

The front wheel is carried on a subframe suspended on coil springs. It turns on a swivel arm mounted in the hub.

Carburettor, crankcase and transmission (left) are normally concealed by a steel casing.

Incredibly low, the Ner-a-car's pressed steel frame encloses the crankcase and front wheel completely. The handlebars have a linkage to connect them to the steering.

# Cotton TT

Built to prove a design principle, the vintage Cottons went on to win two 1920s TTs and score a further seven places as well as launching the career of one of the greatest road racers in history.

Many engineers deplored the traditional motorcycle frame's dependence on inherently weak bent tubes, but few put their ideas into practice. Willoughby Cotton was a law student rather than an engineer, but he succeeded where many others compromised. Before World War I he set out a principle of design in which all tubes were to be straight and fully triangulated. All tubes should be in compression or tension, rather than subjected to bending forces. The design he sketched achieved all these objectives, with the secondary advantages that, as well as strength, it offered lightness and a low centre of gravity.

A prototype was constructed by Levis, but Cotton decided to go into manufacture in his own right. Abandoning his law career, he raised money to establish a factory in Gloucester shortly after the end of the war. As a small factory, entering three machines in the 1922 Isle of Man TT was a bold stroke. Even bolder was offering a ride to an unknown Irishman aged 17. Stanley Woods was an aspiring racer without any real experience, who despite huge adversities, which included himself and the motorcycle catching fire on a stop

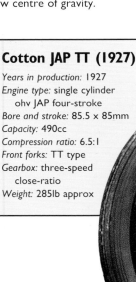

### Cotton JAP TT (1927)

*Years in production:* 1927
*Engine type:* single cylinder ohv JAP four-stroke
*Bore and stroke:* 85.5 x 85mm
*Capacity:* 490cc
*Compression ratio:* 6.5:1
*Front forks:* TT type
*Gearbox:* three-speed close-ratio
*Weight:* 285lb approx

*The straight, triangulated tubes from headstock to rear wheel spindle were the principle on which Cotton was established, clearly visible on this 500cc racer.*

for refuelling, rode a furious race to finish fifth, more than justifying Cotton's faith. The following year he stormed home to win ahead of a field that included the very competitive AJS and Douglas machines. Moving on to other marques, Woods would go on to win a total of 10 TTs, as well as a host of Grands Prix.

Cotton themselves continued to contest the TT throughout the 1920s, and in 1926 took all the first three places in the Lightweight (250cc) race. But such efforts always had to be supported by the manufacture of roadsters, powered by a variety of proprietary engines. After their popularity peaked towards the end of the 1920s, the Depression of the 1930s hit production badly and resulted in falling sales.

With the outbreak of World War 2, motorcycle manufacture was curtailed and Cotton found themselves unable to diversify into other operations. They went into liquidation in 1940.

*The Cotton badge (below) reflected the triangulated principle of the frame, in which all the tubes were braced and subjected only to forces along their length.*

# Sunbeam Model 90

Such were the fine qualities of Sunbeam's roadster models that they were dubbed 'gentleman's motorcycles', but the Model 90, Sunbeam's most sporting machine of the 1920s, was more than capable of holding its own against all comers.

John Marston & Company, the firm that built Sunbeams, was founded in Wolverhampton, as makers of saucepans. In 1890, they began to make bicycles, which gained a reputation for fine finish and durability, as well as a chain enclosure – 'the little oilbath'. Marston's first motorcycle was built in 1912, and was a sound design produced almost entirely in-house. The range expanded, and although not cheap, Sunbeams had a reputation for quality and reliability. After World War 1, during which Sunbeams were used by the Russians and French, production of both singles and V-twin models continued.

The firm began entering reliability trials straight after the war, and re-entered racing soon after. Riding side-valve 500cc machines, Tommy de la Hay won the 1920 TT with team-mate George Dance taking the lap record. In 1922 Alec Bennett won again on a similar machine. Sunbeam had to wait until 1928 for another win, but this time it was their latest overhead-valve model ridden by the diminutive Charlie Dodson that secured them the honours. Although the company had experimented with an overhead-cam design in 1925, the winning machine was Model 90 works-prepared version. Dodson repeated the performance in 1929, with Alec Bennett second on a similar machine.

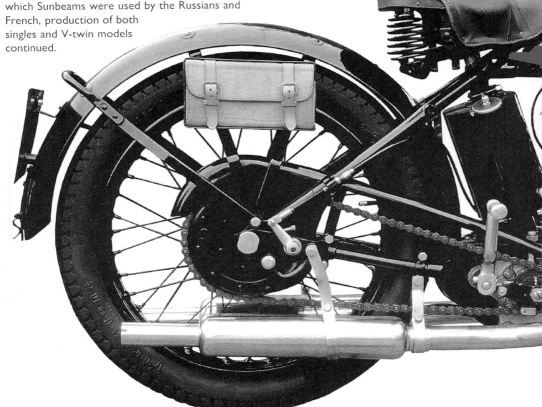

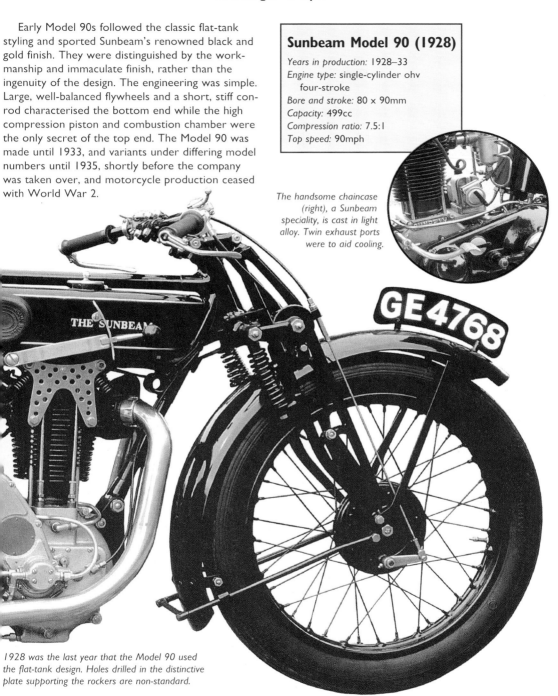

Early Model 90s followed the classic flat-tank styling and sported Sunbeam's renowned black and gold finish. They were distinguished by the workmanship and immaculate finish, rather than the ingenuity of the design. The engineering was simple. Large, well-balanced flywheels and a short, stiff con-rod characterised the bottom end while the high compression piston and combustion chamber were the only secret of the top end. The Model 90 was made until 1933, and variants under differing model numbers until 1935, shortly before the company was taken over, and motorcycle production ceased with World War 2.

## Sunbeam Model 90 (1928)

*Years in production:* 1928–33
*Engine type:* single-cylinder ohv
    four-stroke
*Bore and stroke:* 80 x 90mm
*Capacity:* 499cc
*Compression ratio:* 7.5:1
*Top speed:* 90mph

*The handsome chaincase (right), a Sunbeam speciality, is cast in light alloy. Twin exhaust ports were to aid cooling.*

THE SUNBEAM

GE 4768

*1928 was the last year that the Model 90 used the flat-tank design. Holes drilled in the distinctive plate supporting the rockers are non-standard.*

# Velocette KTT

Throughout the 1920s the Velocette factory won a host of races, thanks to innovative design and great engineering. The overhead-camshaft 'cammy' KTT models swept the board towards the end of the decade, particularly at the Isle of Man TT.

Percy Goodman, the son of the founder, started work on a overhead-camshaft design as early as 1924. However, while it attracted much attention, the prototype was far from a success and the model had to be heavily redesigned after its 1925 racing debut resulted in retirements.

However, in 1926, the design was an almost immediate winner, taking first place in the Junior (350cc) TT. In 1928, it became the first Junior machine to lap the Isle of Man at speeds of more than 70mph, winning eight TTs and Grands Prix.

From mid 1929 the KTT model was available to private owners as a 'race replica' for £80, and in private hands, cammy Velos went on to be the most successful amateur racing machines of the era, filling the first eight places at the Manx Grand Prix (the amateur version of the TT).

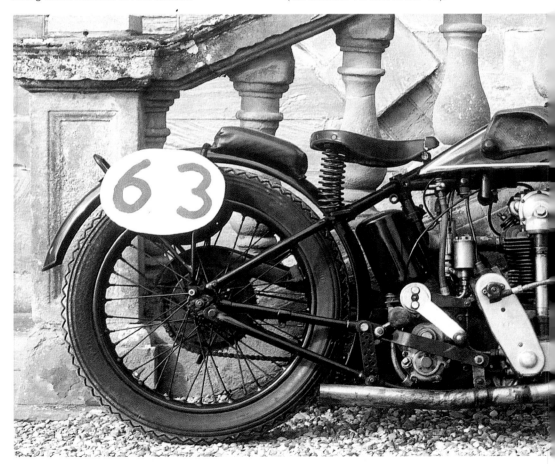

*The alloy casting (left) houses a pair of bevel gears driving the overhead-camshaft via the vertical shaft up the side of the cylinder barrel.*

By then a KTT had also put the world 350cc Hour Speed Record up to 100.39mph – the first time a 350 had topped 100mph. This feat was carried out at Brooklands by Velocette's own designer Harold Willis, one of the most innovative designers of his day.

In an era when cumbersome hand-change levers on the tank were the norm, the advantages of foot-change for racing had been recognised for some time. Several machines sported foot- or knee-change levers so that gears could be selected without letting go of the handlebars. Willis devised the now virtually universal positive-stop gearbox, in which a single movement of the lever automatically selects the next gear up or down; the only limitation on the early KTT was that it retained a three-speed gearbox – changed to a four-speeder in 1932. The positive-stop gearchange was brilliant and helped Velocette to become an even bigger success in competition.

The 'K' series – a model letter that stood for camshaft – developed throughout the 1930s, with variants such as the KSS (Super Sports) and KTS (Touring Sports). (TT of course meant TT replica.)

Mass production of the KTT was discontinued in 1935, but the works racer continued to be developed. After reaching a peak just before World War 2, the KTT series continued after the war with the MkVIII – itself to become a legend.

---

## Velocette KTT (1929)

*Years in production:* 1925–50
*Engine type:* single-cylinder
    overhead-cam four-stroke
*Bore and stroke:* 74 x 81mm
*Capacity:* 348cc
*Compression ratio:* 7.25:1
*Power:* 20bhp

---

*Modified for racing, this KTT originally left the factory in July 1929 and was ridden to fourth place in the Manx Grand Prix that year. The rear subframe, a 1932 type, is a later modification.*

# Norton CS1

By the late 1920s racing had long been a main force behind Norton's development, although the pace of technological change had accelerated rapidly. Until the beginning of the decade the main sporting effort had been carried by the firm's simple side-valvers, but in 1924 it was the new pushrod Model 18 that carried the factory to victory in the first TT since 1907. All that was about to change, for a scant three seasons later, the first of a long line of overhead-camshaft Nortons was to appear.

The CSI, standing for Camshaft One, was the

### Norton CSI (1929)

*Years in production:* 1921–34
*Engine type:* single-cylinder
    side-valve four-stroke
*Bore and stroke:* 79 x 100mm
*Capacity:* 490cc
*Compression ratio:* 7:1
*Power:* 25bhp
*Carburettor:* Amal
*Tyres (front/rear):* 3¼ x 26in
*Top speed:* 85mph

*Low-slung in the frame, the tall Norton CSI engine set the tone for a generation of 'cammy' Nortons after it established its dominance in the 1927 TT.*

*The engine's clean lines and sturdy construction are typically Norton. But where on earlier models the crankcase itself linked the front and rear downtubes, engine and gearbox are carried above a forging that forms the bottom of a cradle frame. The three-speed gearbox has no positive stop, so gear selection requires very careful footwork.*

The bottom end closely followed the traditional Norton design, but cast into the side of the crankcase was a housing for the oil pump and a pair of bevel gears. These drove a long shaft housed in a tube running up the side of the barrel, splined to a second pair of bevel gears driving the overhead-camshaft. The new engine was then fitted into the factory's full cradle frame, which had a separate forging linking the front and rear tubes, housing the three-speed gearbox and the engine. A true saddle tank was fitted, concealing a frame that had to be tall, in order to accommodate the great height of the overhead-camshaft engine.

The new machines were ready for the 1927 TT, an event which they dominated in the hands of works riders Stanley Woods, Joe Craig and Alec Bennett. The next year a 348cc version appeared, and in 1929 was shown as the CJ, Junior model. Although there were few racing honours in either year, the CS continued to show its superiority, and might have continued to do so for many years, were it not for the departure of its creator.

Walter Moore accepted a lucrative offer from the German company NSU, for whom he would create a number of influential machines before he left with the outbreak of war. One of his first designs, however, was so closely based on the CS1, apart from using a four-speed gearbox, that the new 1930 NSU Rennmaschine was jokingly dubbed 'Norton Spares Used'. Moore claimed the original design had been done in his own time, and there was little that Norton could do to prevent him. They rapidly put together an alternative design, while Moore's NSUs were good enough to keep racing until 1935.

brainchild of Walter Moore, a brilliant designer who had joined Norton after stints at Douglas and ABC. Although he had been instrumental in the Model 18, Moore had long favoured the overhead-camshaft layout. After Velocette achieved a win in the 1926 Junior with their new 'cammy' model, and following rumours of other similar developments, Norton got the spur he needed. Taking up a design he had already sketched out, Moore laid down the machine that would carry Norton's works effort in 1927.

# Scott Squirrel

**Scott Squirrel (1928)**

*Years in production:* 1926–40
*Engine type:* Parallel twin-cylinder
  water-cooled two-stroke
*Capacity:* 596cc
*Carburettor:* Binks
*Gearbox:* three-speed with hand chang
*Wheelbase:* 55½in
*Weight:* 325lb
*Top speed:* 70mph

*Handsome and more conventional in appearance than its predecessors, the three-speed Flying Squirrel suffered only from a thirst for fuel and a hefty price tag. Although the frame is still triangulated, the large fuel tank fills the centre of the frame.*

Scott built their reputation by flying in the face of convention. In the pioneer days, their delicate but never frail two-stroke twins were a delightful and effective alternative to the bicycle-framed, girder-forked, four-stroke single norm. But with the death of the founder in 1923 all that began to change. The late vintage Squirrel slid towards a conformity that would eventually lose much of the charm of the originals. At the time, it seemed an attractive answer to satisfying the demands of an increasingly conservative mass market, and was a favourite machine for many competition riders.

The Squirrel name came into being in 1921, on the new 500cc sports model. It was an appropriate name for a cheeky, agile machine that was third in the Senior TT of 1922, made a fastest lap in the 1923 event and was second in 1924. At first, the Squirrel remained true to Alfred Scott's original open frame, two-speed concept. But from 1922, the company began to dabble with a three-speed design, using a conventional gearbox and clutch, and a three-speed Squirrel was shown in 1923. In 1926, the racing version's gearbox was much improved, but more importantly, the frame and forks were completely revamped. The frame was made of heavier tubing, and the fork was extensively braced. There was a top bracing tube, and the tank filled the open frame as on racing machines. The resulting machine had a more conventional appearance, but had gained around one-third in weight. This model was the basis of the roadster Flying Squirrel models that followed. The 500cc machine that appeared at the 1926 Earls Court Show was identical, along with a 600cc option. There was a considerable increase in price, making them around twice the price of a sporty four-stroke.

*The desirable TT Replica of 1930 embodies racing features such as quick-action features and foot-change gearbox, but uses substantially the same mechanical design.*

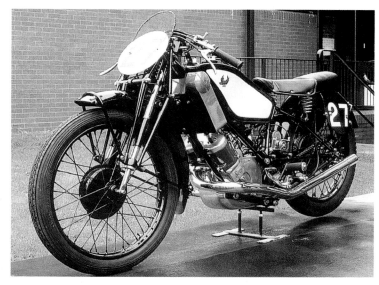

The year 1928 saw Scott's last place in a Senior TT, a third, and towards the end of the season the factory put a Replica on sale. It would become one of the best loved models. As part of a cost-cutting exercise for 1929, which saw the Squirrels drop in price, they also launched a more basic Tourer at under £70.

By 1931 Scott's financial straitjacket and the mounting recession had the firm in great difficulties. There was no entry at the TT, nor the annual motorcycle show. There were detail modifications to the range each year, but the most significant efforts were reserved for a prototype three-cylinder two-stroke. Although this was proudly shown in 1934, Scott lacked resources to exploit the design.

The original Scott went out of production during the war and never really recovered after it. In 1950, the firm was sold to Matt Holder's Aerco company, based in Birmingham. Holder continued to sell bikes from the assets acquired, but it was not until 1956 that a new machine was built. The 'Birmingham Scotts' had a conventional swinging arm frame and a 600cc version of the Scott engine.

The hand-change gate for the gearbox is carried behind the traditional and very effective Scott honeycomb radiator (left).

The front forks, which use a plunger-type suspension, are also heavily braced (right).

# Matchless Silver Hawk

The London-based Matchless company was among Britain's leading companies in the 1930s. Despite the depression it was sufficiently buoyant in 1931 to buy up the ailing AJS concern and merge it into Associated Motor Cycles Ltd (AMC).

In the autumn of the previous year, Matchless had demonstrated its buoyancy to an astonished public by launching an outstanding new model at the Earls Court Show. With a technical specification that reads more like the 1980s than the 1930s, the new machine was a 600cc four-cylinder design with overhead-camshaft, rear-sprung frame and coupled brakes, plus a stylish appearance and sporting performance.

This was not the first time that Matchless had tried such a design – the company's earlier Silver Arrow had a similar layout. Designer Bert Collier, one of the two brothers behind Matchless, had decided to retain the best features of the Silver Arrow but give the sporting public the performance it craved. As on the Silver Arrow, the cylinder casting was in one piece. The crankshaft ran across the frame, and the conrods were offset in two pairs so that the front and rear cylinders could be in line. The overhead-camshaft and valve gear was driven by a shaft taken from one end of the crankshaft.

*The instrument panel (above) was a practical feature borrowed from the earlier Silver Arrow.*

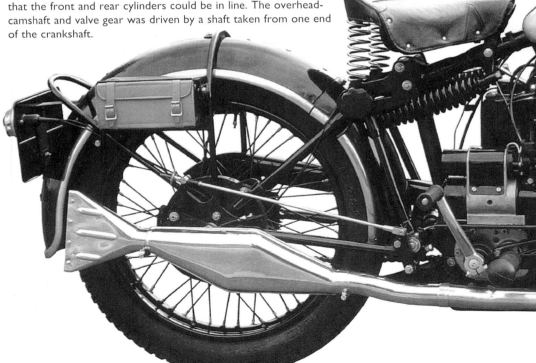

The sporting 600 was fitted to a frame that was virtually the same as the Silver Arrow's. It included a rear fork pivoting on bonded rubber bushes, with a pair of springs and a friction damper under the single saddle. Handsome and stylish, the whole machine was designed very much in the current fashion and looked to have a bright future. The engine was so easy to start, it was

### Matchless Silver Hawk Model B (1934)

*Years in production:* 1931–35
*Engine type:* narrow-angle V-four overhead-cam four-stroke
*Bore and stroke:* 50.8 x 73mm
*Capacity:* 592cc
*Gearbox:* four-speed Sturmey-Archer
*Top speed:* 76mph

said that it could be done by hand. Top speed was more than 80mph. The engine was flexible enough to potter along in top gear, an important consideration of the day when the awkwardness of hand-changing meant that riders liked to stay in top for as long as possible.

Sadly, just as with the Silver Arrow, there were overheating problems. The engine was hard to maintain, although it could be decoked in the frame. Other models, launched at the same time as the Silver Hawk, suffered similar teething problems, overcoming them through design development. But the Hawk proved just too expensive and survived no more than five years. It simply did not offer enough benefits to the limited number of customers who could afford the money to purchase it.

*A handsome example of 1930's styling, the Matchless Silver Hawk had a lively performance and exotic specification.*

# Excelsior Manxman

Excelsior was founded in Coventry in 1874 as a bicycle manufacturer, but well before the turn of the century it had built Britain's first commercial motorcycle. During the pioneer years before World War I, the company produced small numbers of interesting machines, including an 850cc single, and was the first marque to achieve a mile-a-minute in a speed trial.

The firm was taken over by one of its suppliers after World War I, and the new management proved to be the spur to the firm becoming heavily involved in racing, as well as offering a range of everyday lightweight machines powered by proprietary JAP, Villiers or Blackburne engines. Their racing effort led to several successes – and when Excelsior's Syd Crabtree won the Lightweight TT in 1929, the firm offered replicas for sale the very next season.

Rather than use proprietary engines, Excelsior developed their own design, and in 1933 came up with a world beater. A 250cc, designed by Excelsior's Eric Walker and Blackburne's Ike Hatch, it followed Rudge's pioneering four-valve work. Technically advanced but complicated, it used fully radial valves operated by

## Excelsior Manxman (1935)

*Years in production:* 1934–39
*Engine type:* single-cylinder overhead-cam four-stroke
*Bore and stroke:* 63 x 69mm (25 75 x 79mm (350)
*Capacity:* 249cc
*Compression ratio:* 6.5:1
*Cylinder head:* two-valve aluminium-bronze
*Gearbox:* three-speed close-ratio
*Weight:* 280lb

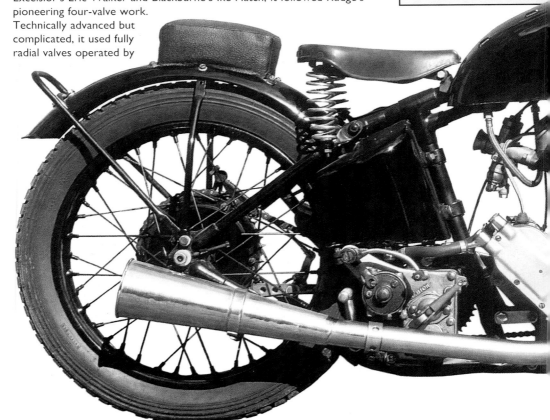

pushrods driven from twin camshafts, and both inlet ports had their own carburettor. Dubbed the 'Mechanical Marvel' this experimental engine won the 1933 Lightweight TT at a record speed in its first outing, despite atrocious weather.

The feat was not to be repeated, however, and in 1935 Walker and Hatch designed the much more conventional Manxman, a two-valve machine using a bevel-driven single overhead-cam. Easier to build than the Mechanical Marvel, it was also very reliable and handled well. The following year, the Manxman gained a four-valve head and took second place in the 1936 and '37 Lightweight TTs, while a 350 version scored a third in the 1937 Junior. More importantly for the company's fortunes, replicas were on sale to privateers, who kept the Manxman's name to the fore in racing for many years to come, while the model was also popular with sporting road riders.

At the TT, Excelsior continued to place each year until war brought an end to racing. In 1938, when they took second and third places, Excelsior used a spring frame, which added to the already good road-holding qualities. The performance was good enough to achieve Lightweight thirds in the first and second post-war events, but the company itself was not to return to the field in which it had once been so strong a contender.

*Bronze head, widely spaced fins and overhead-camshaft (above) are characteristic features of the Manxman.*

*The 250cc Excelsior Manxman was a fitting tribute to Britain's oldest manufacturer.*

# Norton International

Designed by development engineer Joe Craig in association with Arthur Carroll, the Model 30 appeared in 1930. The following year, Norton achieved a host of wins around the world, so the name International was a natural choice for its premier racer. It had neatly trounced the opposition in the Senior TT, a feat repeated by the 350cc in the Junior. In the autumn it took the one-hour record at Montlhéry at more than 110mph.

From 1932 the International that went on sale to the public was effectively a TT replica, equipped with road fittings. The Roadholder forks were made by Norton in place of the Webbs fitted previously, and the frame was shorter and lower than the CS1 had used. Newly designed quickly-detachable wheels were a practical benefit of racing experience, while a large tank with sporting lines became an International hallmark and added greatly to the model's visual appeal.

Above all, it was the engine that defined the International, with a very strong bottom end and massive fly- wheels, the cylinder barrel and head were held by long through bolts. A labyrinthine oil system fed lubricant to the big end, cylinder wall, cambox and valve guides via jets which could be adjusted. Top speed was in the region of 100mph.

Minor improvements followed year-on-year. The forks and gearbox were redesigned in 1933 and from 1935 the gearbox was made by Norton rather than Sturmey-Archer. From 1936 onwards, the racing specification included an alloy cylinder barrel and head with a bronze combustion chamber and aluminium fins.

In 1938, plunger rear springing, as used on the 1937 works racers, was adopted. By this time the Inter, sold with racing fittings, had become very expensive. From 1937, the true works racers had gained a double overhead-camshaft – the first step on the road to the evolution of the Manx Norton. But the Inter itself remained one of the most desirable motorcycles on offer. Production ceased in 1940 with the advent of war – the end of the first chapter in the International's story.

*Tower of power (left): Norton's long-stroke single carries its valve gear in a separate casting bolted to the top of the cylinder head, resulting in a tall engine dominated by the polished tube housing the drive-shaft to the overhead-cam. The head and barrel are in cast-iron, but alloy was an option.*

## Norton International Model 30 (1936)

*Years in production:* 1931–39 (rigid) 1938–39

*Engine type:* single ovh-cam single-cylinder four-stroke

*Bore and stroke:* 79 x 100mm

*Capacity:* 490cc

*Compression ratio:* 7.23:1

*Power:* 29bhp

*Carburettors:* $1^{5}/_{32}$in Amal TT

*Tyres (front/rear):* 3 x 27in/ $3^{1}/_{4}$ x 27in

*Wheelbase:* $54^{3}/_{4}$in

*Top speed:* 93mph

*Girder forks and a rigid rear end are the hallmark of the early Inter. Two years after this model was made, Norton's newly developed plunger rear suspension was adopted.*

# Vincent Rapide

The Vincent motorcycle began and ended with an uncompromising vision: to be faster, more powerful, better at handling, and better all round than anything on the market. The ultimate form of the machine was very much the personal vision of the company's founder, Philip C Vincent. But the company goes back to another man with a personal view of what a motorcycle should be – Howard R Davies.

Davies won the 1921 500cc Senior AT on a 350 AJS, but becoming increasingly disillusioned with the failings of standard products, he founded his own company, HRD, in 1924. The bike was largely an assembly of proprietary parts – JAP engine, Druid or Webb racing forks, Burman gearbox – but he chose the best of everything, and put them together with an expert's know-how. A low seating position and one of the first saddle tanks gave them a sleek appearance and good handling. In 1925 Davies proved his point by winning the Senior TT with one. Always exclusive, HRDs sold in small quantities and foundered financially after just two years and were bought by OK Supreme. Philip Vincent had owned a 1923 BSA the defects of which so incensed him that he decided he could do better. While studying engineering at Cambridge, he built his first prototype when he was only 19 years old. It attracted the attention of the influential editor of *The Motor Cycle*, who suggested that Vincent should purchase a known name, rather than try to attract the public with his radical ideas.

*A proprietary JAP single-cylinder engine was a feature of the original HRD motorcycle. After Philip Vincent bought the name he continued for a time to fit these popular units, although now using a spring frame of his own design (below).*

*Few could argue with the phenomenal performance that resulted from the happy accident of the V-twin's design (right). Scarcely larger or heavier than a single it developed almost twice the power.*

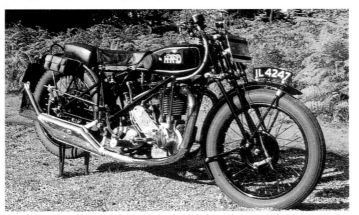

## Vincent Rapide (1937)

*Years in production:* 1936–39
*Engine type:* 47.5° V-twin ohv four-stroke
*Bore and stroke:* 84 x 90mm
*Capacity:* 998cc
*Compression ratio:* 6.8:1
*Power:* 45bhp @ 5500rpm
*Carburettors:* 1¹⁄₁₆in Amals
*Tyres (front/rear):* 3 x 20in/3½ x 19in
*Wheelbase:* 56in
*Weight:* 430lb
*Top speed:* 105+mph

Complexity became an art form in the shape of the Series A Rapide, dating from 1937 (left). The bike had a web of external oil pipes, which led to the model being dubbed a 'Plumber's Nightmare'.

Backed by his father, Vincent took over HRD's assets from OK Supreme in 1928. The first products carried the HRD tank badge, but little else of Davies' designs remained. In place of the neat, stylish singles, Vincent's offerings looked complex and a far cry from the neat diamond familiar to most motorcyclists. Worst of all they were slow to sell.

Matters improved when Vincent met Phil Irving. Supremely practical, Irving possessed the skill and vision to turn Vincent's ideas into a machine that appealed to most riders, while giving it the great performance that would turn heads.

Sales picked up in the early 1930s. In 1936 Vincent took the final step to legendary status. The turning point came when Irving noticed a drawing and a tracing of the 500cc Comet engine lying together. He realised that with few modifications a V-twin could be created, and that it would fit into the single's frame. For just a little extra weight, the difference was phenomenal, producing awesome power through the simple alteration of lining up the single's timing gear. The Series A Rapide could top 110. Some 80 were built before the war. Post-war, they would spawn one of the greats of the British industry.

# Triumph Speed Twin 5T

The Speed Twin changed the face of motorcycling. Before it, most motorcycles, sporting or otherwise, were singles. But the Speed Twin was so successful that almost all other factories jumped on the bandwagon with their own versions. Its parallel twin engine configuration was to endure until the demise of Triumph some four decades later.

One man can take most of the responsibility for the Speed Twin – Edward Turner, who had been the man behind Ariel's Square Four. Moving to Triumph, Turner quickly revitalised the firm's 250, 350 and 500cc singles as the Tiger 70, 80 and 90. Good looks and exciting performance suggested by their name ensured the new models' popularity. However in 1938, Edward Turner brought out the range leader that would really establish Triumph as market leaders.

Turner's new Speed Twin was light and smaller than the Tiger 90, enabling it to slot into the same frame. Weighing 5lb less than the Tiger 90, it cost only £5 more at £75. It had better acceleration, pulled more smoothly and revved more freely, with valve gear many supposed to have been influenced by the sporting Riley cars.

The first Speed Twins had a one piece iron cylinder block with six studs holding the base. This proved a weakness and was soon changed to eight studs. The head was also cast iron. Camshafts in front and behind the crankcase opening drove pushrods between the cylinders, operating the valve gear in separate alloy boxes bolted to the cylinder head.

Ignition and lighting were by a Lucas Magdyno behind the cylinders, and lubrication was by dou-ble-plunger pump. Transmission was by a separate four-speed gearbox. The appealing finish was Amaranth red and chrome with gold lining, the engine was good for around 90mph. In 1939, the factory produced a sports model, the Tiger 100. Finished in black instead of red, this model would top 100mph. Fitted with a supercharger, it took the Brooklands 500cc lap record to over 118mph.

Had it not been for the war, which interrupted production, the trend-setting Speed Twin might have dominated the market even sooner. As it was, it ushered in a period during the 1950s when BSA, Norton and a host of marques such as Royal Enfield and Ariel all followed Triumph down a parallel twin route .

> **Triumph Speed Twin 5T (1938)**
>
> *Years in production:* 1938–40
> *Engine type:* 180° parallel twin ohv four-stroke
> *Bore and stroke:* 63 x 80mm
> *Capacity:* 498cc
> *Compression ratio:* 7.2:1
> *Power:* 27bhp @ 6300rpm
> *Carburettors:* 1in Amal
> *Tyres (front/rear):* 3 x 20in/3¼ x 20in
> *Wheelbase:* 55in
> *Top speed:* 95mph

*Looking almost like a contemporary twin-port single but with a much brisker performance, Triumph's handsome 5T was an instant hit.*

# BSA Gold Star

By 1937, BSA was Britain's largest motorcycle manufacturer, but it had built its reputation on providing good, solid workhorses, rather than racers. After a disastrous outing at the TT in 1921, BSA had turned its back on speed events, preferring to promote the product through reliability trials and other, off-road events.

So it was with some surprise that the Brooklands spectators noted the entry of a BSA 500cc Empire Star in 1937. Even more surprising was the rider, Walter 'Wal' Handley, one of the best racers of the day.

Designer Val Page had made major engine modifications, as well as which, the reliable, but normally sluggish Empire Star had gained a new, much lighter frame. So, in fact, Handley's mount was far from being a standard Empire Star. The riding position was lower and adapted for racing, and it was fitted with a racing carburettor and magneto, plus special gearing. Handley's fastest lap exceeded 107mph and he won the race at more than 102mph.

At Brooklands, anyone who completed a lap at more than 100mph was awarded a special badge bearing a six-pointed star and the number 100 – the 'Gold Star'. It was only natural when BSA decided to capitalise on their success with the launch of a new sporting 500 in 1938, calling it the Gold Star.

## BSA Gold Star (1939)

Years in production: 1938–39
Engine type: single-cylinder ohv
  four-stroke
Bore and stroke: 82 x 94mm
Capacity: 496cc
Compression ratio: 7.8:1
Power: 28bhp @ 5250rpm
Carburettor: Amal TT
Tyres (front/rear): 3 x 20in/
  3½ x 19in
Wheelbase: 54in
Top speed: 92mph

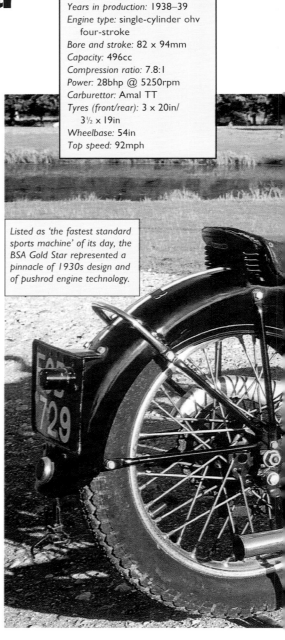

Listed as 'the fastest standard sports machine' of its day, the BSA Gold Star represented a pinnacle of 1930s design and of pushrod engine technology.

Based on the Brooklands trophy that gave the model its name, the BSA's Gold Star badge (above) dominates either side of the handsomely chromed fuel tank.

Listed as the model M24, the Gold Star was fitted with an aluminium head and barrel and a gearbox cast in magnesium alloy. A racing Amal TT carburettor was used and a plain-barrelled silencer replaced the can-type that Brooklands' regulations required. Most of the rest of the machine followed the Empire Star, although both a trials version and a racer were also catalogued.

In fact, Gold Star sales were poorer than expected. But some competition success kept it in production and the next year a modified version appeared.

For 1939, the last year of production before the war, much more handsome in appearance, the new Gold Star was catalogued at £77 as 'the fastest standard sports machine you can buy'. It was the beginning of a model that would become a legend.

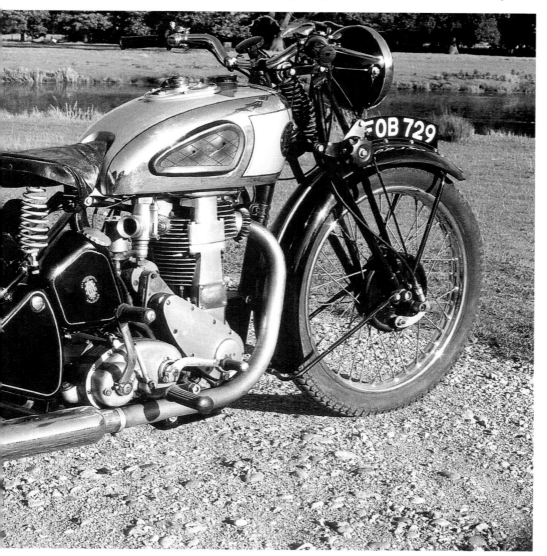

# Rudge Ulster

Rudge Whitworth's final sporting model was named after the race in which it won its greatest victory – the Ulster Grand Prix, billed as the world's fastest motorcycle road race. As it was first offered to the public, the machine was virtually a race replica, although in later years roadster refinements were added.

Rider Graham Walker (later a journalist and father of motorsports commentator Murray) had been appointed Rudge sales manager in 1926. When he took first place in the 1928 Ulster Grand Prix, after an epic battle against rival Charlie Dodson on his Sunbeam Model 90, it was the first time a road race had been won at over 80mph.

Before the year was out, Ernie Nott took the world two-hour record at 100 mph+, and there were further records in 1929. In Grand Prix racing, there were mixed fortunes until 1930, when the first two Senior AT and the first three Junior places all fell to Rudge.

The winning formula was a triumph of technology and engineering.

## Rudge Ulster (1939)

Years in production: 1929–39
Engine type: single-cylinder, four-valve semi-radial overhead-valve four-stroke
Bore and stroke: 85 x 88mm
Capacity: 499cc
Compression ratio: 7.25:1
Brakes: 8in coupled, front & rear
Power: 45bhp @ 5300rpm
Carburettors: 1¹⁄₁₆in Amals
Tyres (front/rear): 2¾ x 21in/ 2¾ x 19in
Top speed: 85mph

The clean lines of Rudge's top sporting roadster – as well as its four-valve engine derive directly from the machine that won the Ulster Grand Prix and many other races of the 1930s.

All three 1930 Junior Rudges were home at more than 70 mph, the first machines to break this speed barrier. It was the last year in which a pushrod machine would win the race, although the Lightweight TT fell to the 250cc version in 1931. As late as 1934, a trio of 250s privately entered by Graham Walker scored a Lightweight hat trick.

*(Below) The 1931 Ulster, shown in racing trim, is small and lithe with a leaner look than the later machine.*

As a result of the factory's racing achievements, the range-leading Sports models were rechristened the Ulster in 1929. Refinements included dry-sump lubrication, a new crankcase and enclosed valves. Later models acquired contemporary styling, while the performance kept pace – 100mph in 1930.

Financial troubles were a constant factor for Rudge. The years 1931 and 1932 saw very poor sales, and in 1933 the company had to halt many of its projects, as well as giving up racing.

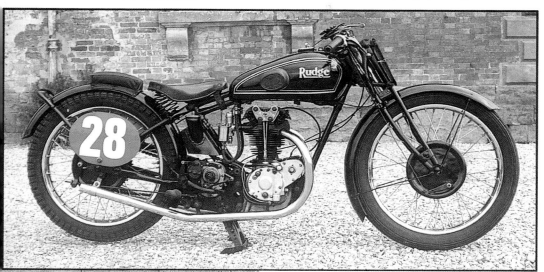

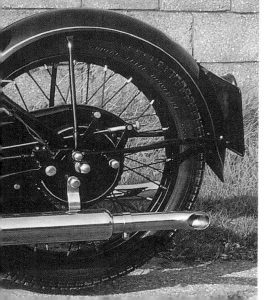

Later that year, Rudge went into receivership, but this was not to be the end, and in 1936 the music and electrical company EMI, a major creditor, took over Rudge. One of the first developments to affect the Ulster and Special model was a new aluminium cylinder head with enclosed valves and revised oil system. During 1937 the factory was moved to EMI's base at Hayes, Middlesex. Sales gradually improved, but it was not enough to save Rudge. With the outbreak of war, EMI had to concentrate on its main business, chiefly the assembly of radio and radar equipment. Although they had intended to resume production when peace came, this was not to be, and in 1943 the Rudge name and tooling were sold off to Raleigh – a sad end to a great pioneering marque.

Manufacturers' badges from 1920 to 1939.

# THE CLASSIC ERA

## 1940–1960

BSA M20 ✪ Excelsior Welbike ✪ AJS 7R
Triumph GP & Trophy ✪ Vincent Rapide
Velocette KTT ✪ LE Velocette ✪ BSA Bantam
Norton Model 18 & ES2 ✪ BSA A10 Golden Flash
Royal Enfield Bullet ✪ Sunbeam S8
Vincent Black Prince ✪ Ariel Square Four
Douglas Dragonfly ✪ Norton Dominator
Velocette MSS ✪ Norton International
BSA Gold Star ✪ Triumph Tiger Cub ✪ Panther M120

# The Classic Era

## Norton in defence and defiance on all fronts

World War 2 meant the end of one era and the beginning of another. Economically, it would sap Britain's reserves and precipitate the break-up of an Empire that had once formed a captive market for British goods, and a cheap source of raw materials. Every available resource had to be mobilised.

Of course this included the motorcycle industry, although not necessarily in the production of motorcycles. Some of Britain's most prestigious names were turned over to making precision parts for the war effort. For the big firms, motorcycle production did continue. BSA produced a stream of 500cc side-valves, the M20, while Norton turned out vast quantities of the similar 16H. Matchless produced the lightweight 350cc overhead-valve G3 with 'Teledraulic' telescopic forks.

Of the major makers, only Triumph was not involved in wartime production, because early in the Coventry blitz, their factory was completely destroyed. Other factories made machines in smaller numbers, including the specialised light-weight folding bikes from Royal Enfield and Excelsior, which were designed to be landed with paratroops. Norton made a Big Four-powered sidecar outfit designed as a gun platform, adopting an ingenious sidecar wheel drive to make it capable of negotiating rough terrain.

*Norton's Big Four driven-wheel sidecar outfit (above) was capable of impressive off-road performance, but was deemed so hazardous to drive under normal conditions that the sidecar wheel drive had to be removed before any were sold off as Army surplus.*

*On active service (left): the military motorcycle, typified by BSA's M20 and Norton's 16H side-valve performed essential service in many theatres of war. But although wartime proved the technical spur for advances in aviation and other fields, most service bikes were based on worthy but basic pre-war designs.*

*In the immediate post-war period there was a massive demand for transport, yet motorcycles and the petrol to power them were both in short supply. Autocycles, precursors of the modern moped, provided one answer.*

The main use of the Allied military machines was, as in World War 1, as despatch and convoy escorts. Over 400,000 British WD bikes were made, and thousands of riders were trained to use them.

When peace returned, as in World War I there was an immediate demand for transport. This time, there were many more experienced riders who were hungry for machines, and as before the demand was met with a mixture of reconditioned ex-service bikes, second-hand machines and finally a trickle of new models.

Many materials were in short supply, but the chief disadvantage for the ordinary rider was the rationing of petrol. Supplies of a low octane 'Pool' petrol began in mid 1945, but private owners were restricted to three gallons a week, or two for machines under 250cc.

New models were not long in coming. Triumph, courtesy of a new factory, was first in production with a post-war range of parallel twins. BSA and AMC rapidly followed suit. However, for many, the route on to two wheels was via an autocycle, fore-runner of the moped, or even a bicycle assisted by a clip-on motor.

Within a year of peace there were half a million bikes in use, nearly double the 1939 total, despite being more expensive, thanks in part to the new purchase tax imposed during the war. As a result the machines that most people were riding were extremely basic and in a low state of tune. Wartime experience had made most machines reliable, but many of the commonest conveniences were still considered extra items such as pillion seats and footrests, air filters and speedometers.

The mood, though, was one of optimism. There were bright ideas aplenty, including some, such as BSA's Bantam and Sunbeam's S7, that were copied from, or inspired by, successful enemy designs. Competition riding had returned as early as June 1945. At the same time, a new movement was

*Despite postwar austerity, there was still room for the superlative, such as the Vincent Black Shadow, amply able to prove that it was the world's fastest.*

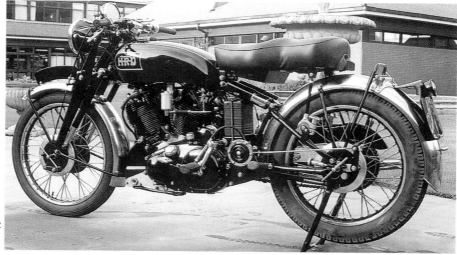

*Motorcycle production boomed throughout the 1950s, buoyed up by an eager home market and healthy export business.*

was under way, with the formation in 1946 of the Vintage Motorcycle Club to ensure that older machines were valued and preserved. Major competitions began to return that year with the first post-war Manx Grand Prix.

The winner of the Senior race proved prophetic. Ernie Lyons was mounted on a new Triumph twin, with a specially developed alloy engine. Over the next few years, the type would become the staple diet of the British industry.

Many of the technical improvements of the pre-war racers had centred around supercharging. Such 'artificial aids' were now banned by the sport's organising bodies and, as a result, several of the British industry's most promising designs lost their advantage. Post-war racing tended to centre on the single cylinder overhead-cam Manx Norton, with similar offerings from AMC and Velocette making up the field. Occasional exotic designs such as the AJS 'Porcupine' surfaced, but despite the undoubted success of the singles, there was little with a technology that could challenge the four-cylinder Italian racers soon being fielded by Gilera, or the technically advanced Moto Guzzi singles.

As the 1940s turned into the 1950s, things still looked good, however. The British industry was booming, with exports at record levels. British bikes were winning races and setting records, with machines such as the exclusive Vincent twins setting the standard by which all others were judged.

There were still shortages, however. With petrol supplies settling down, the Korean War meant that chroming had to be restricted, resulting in a couple of years of painted rims. Behind the scenes the British factories were suffering from a shortage of real investment. The German factories, were coming out with machines that formed the basis for their own post-war expansion, as well as the model for Japan to do the same.

*Many famous names failed to reappear after the war and many succumbed soon after it, including Douglas, which soldiered on for a scant 10 years. Despite the attraction of models such as the much-prized 90 Plus, chronic under-investment would eventually prove the downfall of the company.*

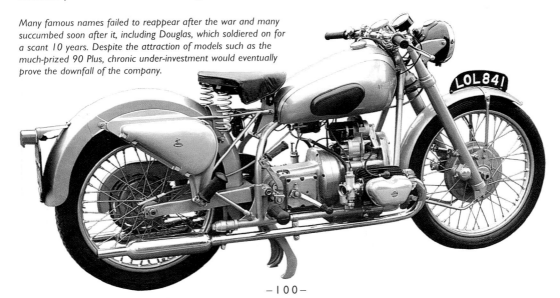

*Throughout the 1950s, motorcycle dealerships were exclusively British offering a range of machines from Ariel, BSA, Excelsior, Matchless, Royal Enfield, Scott and Triumph.*

Italy was offering a host of new ideas, including the scooter. The Vespa, launched in 1946, would spawn a European boom in which British offerings were too little, too late. The Italian scooter was poorly understood in Britain at the time and all too-easily dismissed. In 1953, motorcycles topped the million mark. Britain was the largest motorcycle producer outside the Iron Curtain countries, and in a position to dictate its own terms. This would mask for a few years the advances in engineering design that had been made by the continental opposition, and not just in the field of racing.

This was not to say that British machines did not still lead the world. One only had to look at the competitive records achieved by machines such as the Triumph twins, BSA's Gold Star, the Manx Norton, the AJS 7R and the racing Velocettes to see that, while machines such as the Vincent were still offering a performance that no rivals could match. But there were also external factors that were affecting the market for the British industry's products. In the early 1950s, motorcycles were still everyday transport, for prosperity had still not improved to the degree where cars had become affordable by the mass market. Lightweights were providing commuters with a ride to work, while sidecars were still commonplace family vehicles. But all this was changing, and at a pace that was too fast for most of the British industry to perceive.

Light cars such as the Mini were developed, at a price that would soon challenge the family sidecar, while offering far greater convenience. Italian racing bikes had now espoused streamlining, offering still greater speed potential. Sales of two-wheelers were going up, but many of them were scooters. By the end of the decade motorcycle sales had reached a peak that had not been seen for 30 years. But in truth there were troubles behind the scenes. In Britain, the image of the motorcycle, as well as its economic position, was altering fast.

What had been accepted as family transport a decade before was now increasingly associated with the youth market. The image of the motorcycle outlaw portrayed by Marlon Brando in the banned 1953 film *The Wild One*, had provided a model for suburban rebels across Britain. With the ready availability of cheap, fast and raw machines from all the British factories, the scene was set for a major shift in the attitude of the public to motorcycling.

Technologically, things were also changing fast. While the last 1950s TT was dominated by the Italian MVs and the British Nortons, that year's competition also saw the debut of Honda – and a new challenge to British industry.

# BSA M20

When World War 2 began, BSA was Britain's major motorcycle factory, with the proud boast that 'one in four is a BSA'. The firm had supplied the armed forces in World War I, and as befitted a company that began as an armament manufacturer, had geared up to produce munitions as early as 1935. They would go on to become the biggest supplier of motorcycles to the forces, in the unlikely form of their model M20.

Originally launched in 1937, mainly as a sidecar model, the M20 used a 500cc side-valve engine in a heavy frame. BSA had been supplying the War Office with a variety of models for evaluation, and in some cases purchase, since the late 1920s. The company originally submitted the M20 in 1936, only to see it fail, owing to heavy engine wear. Resubmitted the next year, it passed, and a small batch was purchased in 1938.

The War Office then issued an official policy that favoured the machines already in service, whose reliability was well known, principally the Norton 16H and M20. Large quantities of the BSA model were bought. Heavy, bulky, slow and with limited ground clearance, the M20 had far from an ideal specification, but it was rugged, generally reliable and was easily repaired. Special fittings included a long, spiked prop-stand for field use and a large headlamp, fitted with a blackout mask. In 1942, a shortage of rubber led to rubber hand grips being replaced with canvas fittings and footrests with simple metal ribs. A large air filter mounted on the tank and coupled to the carburettor by a hose was fitted for use in climates such as the African desert. As a result part of the rear of the tank had to be cut away.

Comprising details from various years between 1940–42, this BSA M20 is typical of WD models that were rebuilt many times, losing their original identity in the process.

The M20 used BSA's heavyweight girder forks (left), here liberally finished in khaki paint.

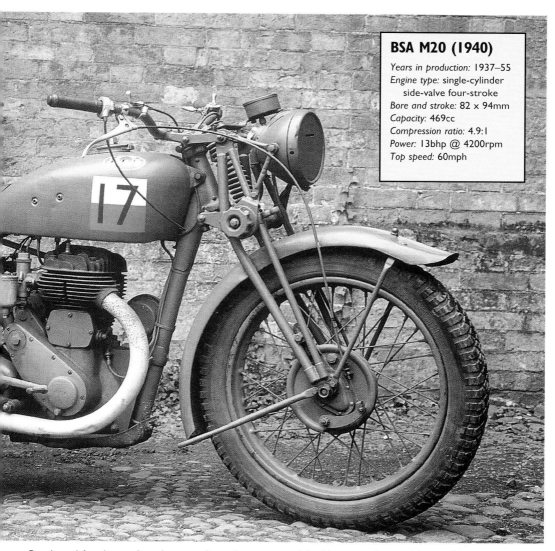

## BSA M20 (1940)

*Years in production:* 1937–55
*Engine type:* single-cylinder
    side-valve four-stroke
*Bore and stroke:* 82 x 94mm
*Capacity:* 469cc
*Compression ratio:* 4.9:1
*Power:* 13bhp @ 4200rpm
*Top speed:* 60mph

Purchased for despatch and escort duty, the M20 served in many theatres of war. Over 125,000 were purchased by the armed forces. The finish consisted largely of applying khaki paint liberally, including the engine, tyres and even the saddle, with different camouflage schemes in various countries.

Vast numbers of M20s were discharged at the end of hostilities, and after gaining a new coat of paint they were snapped up by a transport-hungry public. However the model stayed in service in smaller numbers for many years in some cases as late as 1971. The vast quantities built mean that ex-WD M20s are still in use in many parts of the world, and it is even possible to find that new spares are still available. The civilian model was manufactured until 1955, with its 600cc cousin the M21 soldiering on until 1963, the last side-valve built in Britain.

# Excelsior Welbike

The Excelsior Welbike was an ingenious oddity that grew out of the special needs of wartime. Intended to be dropped by parachute or landed by glider as front line transport for the Airborne Forces, the machine had to be cheap, lightweight, small and expendable.

The motorcycle to fit the bill was not designed by the Excelsior factory themselves. An established engineering concern, Excelsior could lay claim to being the first British maker of motorcycles for sale to the public, but was never a major manufacturer. In fact, at the beginning of the war the factory had undertaken contract engineering rather than motorcycle production.

The prototype was produced at the military research centre in Welwyn in Hertfordshire – hence the name, *Wel*-bike. Its designer began with a standard airborne equipment container and sketched a miniature motorcycle with handlebars and saddle that folded to fit inside. Powered by a 98cc two-stroke Villiers autocycle engine, there was no suspension, no lights and only one brake, the bare minimum necessary. The tiny fuel tank had to be pressurised by pump. To ready the Welbike for use, the handlebars swung up and out until they locked; the saddle pulled up and the footrests pushed down until they locked.

*1943: a paratrooper unpacks the lightweight Welbike, which has been dropped in the special container shown.*

*An early Welbike with a 98cc Villiers autocycle engine. Rubber shortages led to the use of brass and canvas handlebar grips seen here. Also clearly visible is the pump for pressurising the fuel tank.*

Excelsior was contracted to build the machine, and after some refinements it went into production with Excelsior's own 98cc autocycle engine. As planned, the Welbike could be made very cheaply and quickly.

Almost 4000 were built and saw action in parachute drops as well as beach assaults from 1942 until the end of the war. However, its low performance, especially over rough terrain in the heat of battle was seen as a drawback. As a result many saw more use as airfield transport than on the front line.

After the war some were sold off – although, without a front brake, they could not legally be used. Meanwhile the original designer had been developing a civilian version, which was built and sold as the Corgi. It soon proved too slow and unrefined and was discontinued – although the concept returned with the folding Honda 'monkey bikes' of the 1960s and 70s.

Meanwhile Excelsior continued production of their own autocycle and later built a popular two-stroke 250cc twin, the Talisman. The firm survives today as the makers of Britax accessories.

## Excelsior Welbike (1939)

*Frame:* twin loop tubular with folding handlebar and telescopic seat tube
*Suspension:* none
*Gearbox:* none – single speed
*Engine type:* two-stroke, petroil lubricated
*Capacity:* 98cc
*Ignition:* flywheel magneto
*Lighting (on Corgi):* 6 volt dynamo in flywheel magneto
*Wheels:* 10in, 20 psi front, 35 psi rear

# AJS 7R

Known as the 'Boy Racer', the 350cc AJS 7R was one of the most successful club racing machines of its time – dominating the amateur Manx Grand Prix for many years. It is directly related to the 500cc Matchless G50 that came to be a major force in classic racing decades later.

Well before World War 2, AJS had successfully developed the R7 model, which used a tensioned chain drive to its overhead-camshaft. Although the firm had been absorbed by Matchless and become part of Associated Motorcycles Ltd (AMC), when the 7R appeared in 1948 it bore many similarities to the earlier design. Although it was accused of being a copy of Velocette's KTT model, sharing the Velo's dimensions, the valve drive was again by chain, rather than shaft as on the KTT, and the 7R had a modern frame with welded construction and telescopic fork – AMC had pioneered the use of such technology with the much-copied wartime Teledraulic fork. Many castings were in light alloy, including magnesium, which was used extensively. As a result the 7R was much lighter than the KTT, and looked more like a post-war design rather than an update of a pre-war machine.

The year 1948 was not perhaps the best time to launch a performance machine, for the low-octane petrol restriction of the time stifled performance. It was four years before the 7R demonstrated the

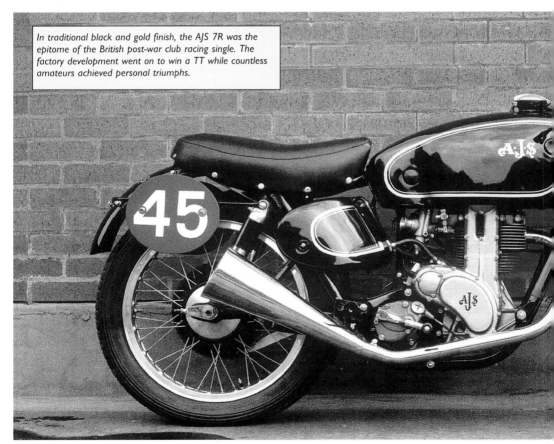

*In traditional black and gold finish, the AJS 7R was the epitome of the British post-war club racing single. The factory development went on to win a TT while countless amateurs achieved personal triumphs.*

force that it would become, with a win in the 1952 Junior (350cc) Manx Grand Prix by rider Bob McIntyre, who trumped this with second place in the 500cc race.

AJS development engineer Jack Williams then took a hand, using gas flow experiments to help develop a much more efficient head design, together with an improved cam and valve setup. These ultimately took the power up by nearly 15 per cent, and the weight down by some 8 per cent by late 1954, turning the machine into a potent racing force.

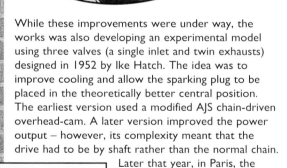

*The distinctive gold-finished chaincase (right) for the drive to the overhead-camshaft, was fitted with a Weller blade tensioner.*

While these improvements were under way, the works was also developing an experimental model using three valves (a single inlet and twin exhausts) designed in 1952 by Ike Hatch. The idea was to improve cooling and allow the sparking plug to be placed in the theoretically better central position. The earliest version used a modified AJS chain-driven overhead-cam. A later version improved the power output — however, its complexity meant that the drive had to be by shaft rather than the normal chain.

Later that year, in Paris, the three-valve AJS machine took a total of five world records. Two years later, in 1954, the team's efforts paid off when AJS won the Junior TT, thus ending a period of four Norton wins. Sadly, the works abandoned this machine soon after, leaving the successful two-valve as the mainstay of a racing effort that sustained hundreds of privateers long after the factory itself had ceased production.

## AJS 7R (1948)

*Years in production:* 1948–54
*Engine type:* single-cylinder single overhead-cam four-stroke
*Bore and stroke:* 74 x 81mm
*Capacity:* 348cc
*Compression ratio:* 10.8–12.2:1
*Power:* 37bhp @ 7500rpm – 42bhp @ 7800rpm
*Weight:* 285lb
*Top speed:* 102mph

# Triumph GP and Trophy

Before World War 2, Triumph laid the foundation of the sporting parallel twin with its innovative Speed Twin. A decade later, the company's racing machines showed the high-speed potential of the format and confirmed its post-war popularity.

Triumph might have been expected to play a major part in the war, but the bombing raids on Coventry so damaged the factory that it was only able to resume limited production during 1942 at temporary premises in Warwickshire. Triumph intended to concentrate its military production on a 350cc machine based on the Speed Twin, but the only model built in quantity was a 350cc single.

Production of the Speed Twin and Tiger 100 resumed in 1945, and these models were soon modernised with telescopic forks. Shortly after, Triumph staff realised that the left-over stock of cylinder barrels from an auxiliary generator unit

Triumph had built for the Air Ministry during the war offered the potential to create a lightweight, high-performance Tiger 100. Specifically providing a means of curing the overheating, to which highly tuned Triumph twins were prone.

Prototypes were prepared by Freddie Clarke, a pre-war record-breaker, and one was entered in the 1946 Manx Grand Prix, ridden by Ernie Lyons. The model achieved a famous win ahead of the Manx Norton. The race machine produced between 25 and 30 per cent more power than the sports roadster, and went into limited production. The generator-based engine was housed in a rigid frame with Triumph's telescopic fork. A form of rear springing was offered by the Turner designed sprung-hub which provided a limited degree of movement, but it was also prone to rapid wear, which could result in severe handling problems.

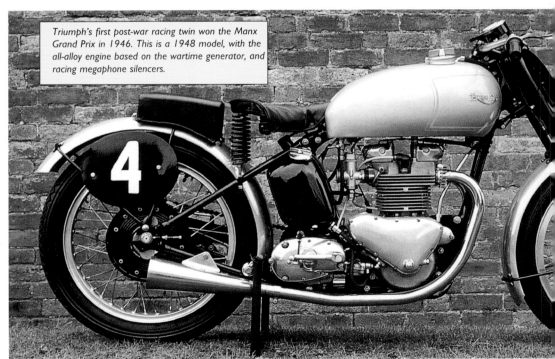

*Triumph's first post-war racing twin won the Manx Grand Prix in 1946. This is a 1948 model, with the all-alloy engine based on the wartime generator, and racing megaphone silencers.*

Despite this, in 1948 the GP model, as it was called, won the Manx Grand Prix again, and over the next few years made its mark in road racing. It was phased out in 1950, making way for race-kitted versions of the T100, but it had already become part of the Triumph legend.

There was another side to the story. In 1948, Triumph had entered an official team in the International Six Days' Trial in Italy, and had created three special ultra-lightweight twin-machines which swept all before them and scooped the manufacturer's award.

In honour of the event Triumph launched a special model – the TR5 Trophy. A versatile, dual purpose machine, this used a single carburettor in place of the roadster's twin-carb setup, and the engine was much more softly tuned. Club riders could use it as everyday transport, and at the weekend remove the headlamp in minutes and be competitive in any form of off-road competition.

*No larger than a contemporary off road single but with a much brisker performance, Triumph's handsome Trophy model was an instant hit.*

## Triumph GP/TR5 (1948–58)

Years in production: 1948–50 GP),
  1948–58 (TR5)
Engine type: 180 degree parallel
  twin ohv four-stroke
Bore and stroke: 63 x 80mm
Capacity: 498cc
Compression ratio: 6:1 (TR5)
Power: 40 bhp (GP), 25bhp
  (TR5) @ 6000rpm
Carburettors: Amal Mk 6
Tyres (front/rear): 3 x 20in/4 x 19in
Wheelbase: 53in
Weight: 295lb (TR5)
Top speed: 85mph (TR5)

# Vincent Rapide

Power and speed: it's a formula that sells superbikes today, although in the grim period of post-war austerity few could afford such luxuries. But who could resist the pull of a one litre machine that advertised itself as 'The World's Fastest Standard Motorcycle'? Phil Vincent and his designer Phil Irving had begun to plan the successor to their Series A Rapide as early as 1943, working on their ideas after hours, or when the Stevenage factory's war work schedule permitted. The machine was to be a 1000cc high-speed, ultra-reliable touring bike.

The layout of the engine was similar to that of the 'Plumber's Nightmare' Series A, but cleaned up with unit construction and smooth alloy castings. Even so, the power unit was still slightly longer than before. To make the bike itself more compact, Irving and Vincent came up with a radical solution. The engine and gearbox unit was so massive and rugged that they could do away with the frame. This had the double advantage

## Vincent Rapide (1948)

*Years in production:* 1946–50
*Engine type:* 50 degree V-twin ohv four-stroke
*Capacity:* 998cc
*Bore and stroke:* 84 x 90mm
*Compression ratio:* 6.45:1
*Power:* 45bhp @ 5300rpm
*Carburettor:* 1 1/16 Amals
*Tyres (front/rear):* 3 x 20in/ 31 x 19in
*Wheelbase:* 56½in
*Top speed:* 110mph

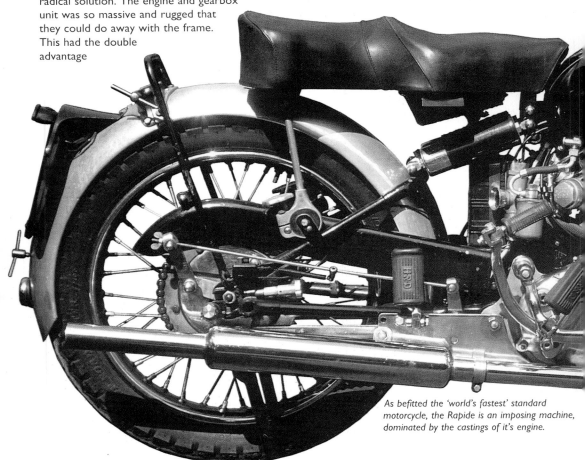

*As befitted the 'world's fastest' standard motorcycle, the Rapide is an imposing machine, dominated by the castings of it's engine.*

that there was no need for the conventional frame tubing that was then in short supply. Instead of a frame, the rear swinging arm pivoted directly behind the gearbox, while on top of the engine a sheet steel box was bolted, which formed an attachment for the rear suspension and the steering head for the front forks. Cleverly, it also doubled as the oil tank.

The forks were conventional Brampton girders, which would later be replaced with Vincent's own design. The twin drum brakes of the Series A remained – at first with steel drums, later with alloy. Convenience was also a feature of the design.

Footrests and pedals were adjustable to suit the length of riders' legs; a dual seat had a linkage that allowed it to move independently; the kickstart could be fitted to either side of the bike; tommy bars were fitted to the wheels so they could be removed with a minimum of tools.

The new Rapide was launched sensationally in 1946. Vincent claimed 45bhp for the engine and 110 mph, a staggering speed for those days.

Two years later, Vincent topped even this, launching the legendary Black Shadow. With 10hp more than the Rapide it delivered a performance of 125mph. Excellent brakes, roadholding and steering made it one of the world's most desirable motorcycles, particularly after Rollie Free took one to a world record of over 150mph at Bonneville Salt Flats in 1948.

A legend was born.

# Velocette KTT

Velocette's enormously successful KTT series had been developed for 14 years when the MkVIII appeared at the Earls Court Show in 1938. Priced at £120, the model was another 'race replica' in the great Velocette tradition and included a host of innovations seen on the works machines that had won that year's Junior TT.

With lightweight alloy parts, sophisticated oiling and a pioneering suspension design, it showed all the benefits of development by a consistent pro-gramme of racing. The most notable feature of the engine was its massive cylinder head casting, with its squared-off light alloy fins virtually filling the frame. Introduced on works racers in 1937 and sold to

the public as a limited run of Mk VII KTTs early in 1938. Similar finning extended to the rocker box, which contained a labyrinth of oilways to lubricate the bevel gears and cams.

The Mk VII had a fairly modest state of tune (with an 8.75:1 compression ratio) and a rigid frame with few special fittings. The Mk VIII was altogether a different proposition. It featured 'swinging-arm' rear suspension and Dowty oleo pneumatic rear shock absorbers, in which the springing was by air under pressure, with oil damping. It had lightweight magnesium alloy brake hubs and a telescopic housing for the front fork spring, while the

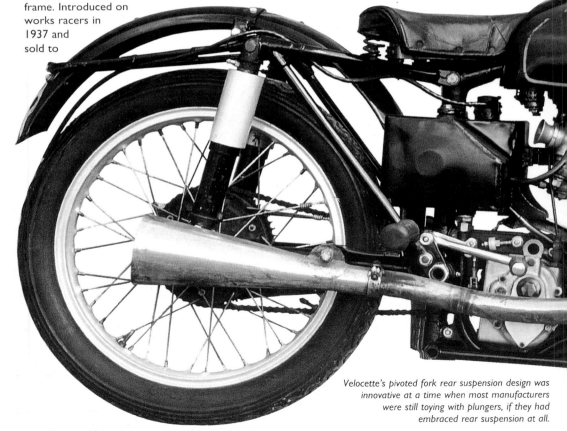

*Velocette's pivoted fork rear suspension design was innovative at a time when most manufacturers were still toying with plungers, if they had embraced rear suspension at all.*

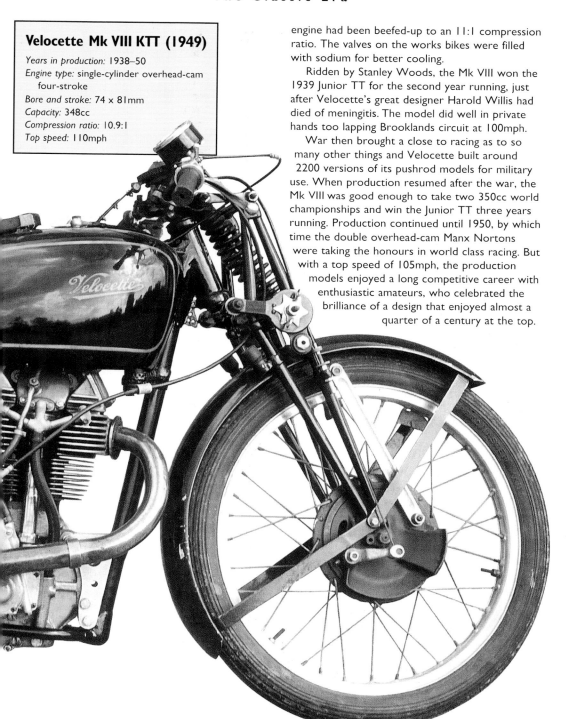

## Velocette Mk VIII KTT (1949)

*Years in production:* 1938–50
*Engine type:* single-cylinder overhead-cam
  four-stroke
*Bore and stroke:* 74 x 81mm
*Capacity:* 348cc
*Compression ratio:* 10.9:1
*Top speed:* 110mph

engine had been beefed-up to an 11:1 compression ratio. The valves on the works bikes were filled with sodium for better cooling.

Ridden by Stanley Woods, the Mk VIII won the 1939 Junior TT for the second year running, just after Velocette's great designer Harold Willis had died of meningitis. The model did well in private hands too lapping Brooklands circuit at 100mph.

War then brought a close to racing as to so many other things and Velocette built around 2200 versions of its pushrod models for military use. When production resumed after the war, the Mk VIII was good enough to take two 350cc world championships and win the Junior TT three years running. Production continued until 1950, by which time the double overhead-cam Manx Nortons were taking the honours in world class racing. But with a top speed of 105mph, the production models enjoyed a long competitive career with enthusiastic amateurs, who celebrated the brilliance of a design that enjoyed almost a quarter of a century at the top.

# LE Velocette

One of a number of post-war designs aimed at producing everyday transport for everyman, the LE Velocette owed little to convention and featured many interesting concepts. But although it enjoyed a production run of some 16 years, like all its peers that dared to be different, the little Velocette was ultimately unsuccessful, never meeting its maker's optimistic sales target.

In the early post-war years, the bulk of Velocette's production consisted of updated versions of their pre-war pushrod models, the MSS and MOV. But in 1948 the firm unveiled the new design that would take their place. Literally, for the model that Velocette were introducing was designed for mass production, and building it needed all the space the factory could provide.

Its design owed little to anything that had been seen before. The 'frame' was a pressed steel box, which offered the same advantages that had been seen in the car industry, of quick, cheap and strong construction – albeit with the disadvantages that it was costly to tool up and difficult to change design.

The telescopic forks and the rear swinging-arm suspension were state-of-the art, with shock absorber units that could be moved in curved upper mounting slots to change the spring rate and damping – a Velocette patent.

Cleanliness and convenience were important features of the design, which was intended to appeal to people who would not consider a conventional motorcycle. Voluminous mudguards, built-in legshields and footboards looked after the cleanlines, while convenience included built-in luggage capacity, a hand starter lever (matched by a hand gearchange on the early models), and shaft drive housed in one leg of the swinging arm.

The model name LE stood for 'little engine'. Just 149cc when it first appeared, the Velocette fitted most of its designers' objectives, but although the engine was easy to start, its performance was decidedly limited. In 1950 the LE was redesigned. It now had a 192cc engine, with some internal modifications, developing 8bhp.

### LE Velocette (1950)

*Years in production:* 1948–68 (variants including Valiant and Vogue)
*Engine type:* horizontally-opposed side-valve four-stroke twin
*Bore and stroke:* 50 x 49mm
*Capacity:* 192cc
*Power:* 8 bhp @ 5000 rpm
*Top speed:* 52mph

Sales were slow, and what kept the LE in production for so long was its appeal to the police, who found it a perfect choice for urban patrol work. This led to the nickname 'Noddy' bike, supposedly as the result of a directive that police patrolmen meeting a superior officer should nod rather than salute, which would have meant taking a hand off the handlebars.

A luxury version, called the Vogue, failed to catch on – a fate that also befell the Valiant in 1956. The LE was sold in small numbers into the 1960s, but long before this, the disappointing sales had forced Velocette to return to building conventional motorcycles, a range that would outlast the LE by over a decade, although the last police 'Noddy' bikes remained in service until 1971.

*A motorcycle for everyman, the Velocette LE offered comprehensive weather protection and luggage space, allied to easy starting and a whisper-quiet engine.*

# BSA Bantam

**BSA Bantam (1951)**

*Years in production:* 1948–63
*Engine type:* piston-ported
  two-stroke single
*Bore and stroke:* 52 x 28mm
*Capacity:* 123cc
*Compression ratio:* 6.5:1
*Power:* 4.5bhp @ 5000rpm
*Top speed:* 50mph

One of the most successful lightweights produced in Britain, the Bantam was actually 'borrowed' from a pre-war German design.

Before World War 2 the German manufacturer DKW was one of the great innovators of two-stroke technology. Until then most two-strokes had used a cumbersome 'defector piston'. DKW's version used a symmetrical, flat-top piston – together with clever transfer porting – to direct the gas flow for better power and reliability. As part of the reparations of war, German designs were offered to the Allies. One such was the DKW RT125. The design was turned down by Villiers, but was rapidly adopted by BSA. The same design was also taken up by the other Allies. Harley-Davidson, Voskhod and WSK all made their own variants – in the latter cases, for decades later. Even Yamaha borrowed the design.

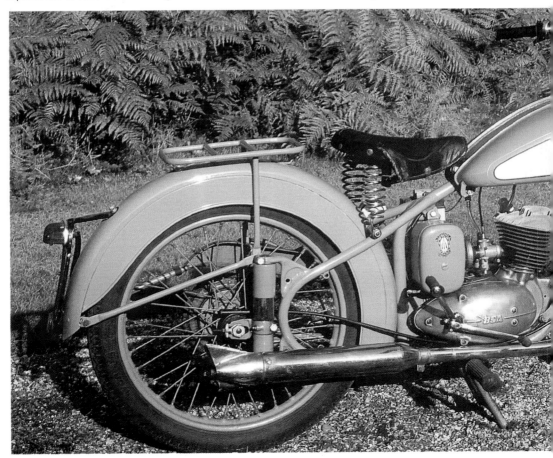

*The neat egg-shaped 123cc power unit (right) with a three-speed gearbox and a flywheel magneto.*

Although the original design had the gearchange on the left in European, rather than British fashion, BSA simply reversed the drawings to make a mirror image of the DKW with a 'conventional' gearchange. Inside the egg-shaped engine castings was a three-speed gearbox in unit with the engine, which had a pressed-up full-circle flywheel. The capacity was 123cc. Lubrication was by petroil mix, fed by a tiny carburettor with integral air filter. Ignition and lighting were by a Wipac flywheel magneto fitted to the left of the crankshaft. Lighting was direct, with no battery fitted.

The new BSA was announced early in 1948, and initially called the D1 it was going to be supplied as a proprietary engine unit only. By October, it had gained the Bantam name. Producing 4$\frac{1}{2}$bhp, it was good for about 50mph on a miserly 120mpg, and despite its £260 price tag, the model sold as fast as BSA could produce it. A version designed for trials or scrambles was also catalogued, while some owners modified machines for lightweight racing.

In 1950 the Bantam was improved and updated with an optional plunger rear suspension. In 1954 a larger 150cc version called the D3 was introduced. It had heavier forks, plunger springing as standard, and a larger front brake, among minor variations. It gained a new swinging-arm frame in 1956, but this was dropped in 1957.

The Bantam continued in production until August 1963, with only a few minor adjustments to electrics, engine and frame. It sold some 20,000 a year and was much-loved by owners all around the world. A workhorse whose duties included telegram deliveries, commuting and farming in the Australian bush. Examples soldiered on for more than a decade as a mainstays of some rider training schemes. Meanwhile, derivatives of the original would continue to be produced as late as 1971.

*Plunger rear springing added comfort to the original D1's rigid rear end, but both front and rear suspension remained undamped except by friction.*

# Norton Model 18 & ES2

## Norton Model 18 & ES2 (1947/52)

*Years in production:* 1921–54 (Model 18), 1928–63 (ES2)

*Engine type:* single-cylinder side-valve four-stroke

*Bore and stroke:* 79 x 100mm

*Capacity:* 490cc

*Compression ratio:* 6.45:1

*Power:* 21bhp

*Carburettor:* Amal Monobloc 276 (1947 Model 18)

*Ignition:* Magneto (prior to 1958)

*Weight:* 374 lb (1947 Model 18)

*Top speed:* 78mph

Pushrod Norton singles date back to 1922, but their heyday really began in 1924 when they carried the factory to a string of race victories. That role was to last a scant three years, supplanted by the more efficient overhead-cam racers. But as roadsters they would continue until 1963, gradually outclassed in the performance stakes, but offering occasional reminders of their sporting heritage.

The Model 18 was the first pushrod Norton, but it adopted a bottom end and 79 x 100mm that went back to the dawn of the marque. It was followed by a host of variants, including the 600cc Model 19 and sports ES2. The origin of the latter model number is uncertain; one theory is that it stands for 'Enclosed Springs', as the first Model 18 had exposed pushrod and return springs.

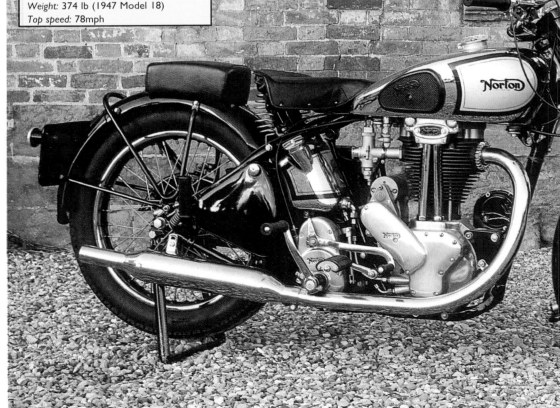

The ES2 (above) shared its heritage and most of its fittings with the Model 18. On the immediate post-war models, the most obvious difference between the two was the ES2's plunger rear suspension.

Post-war the Model 18 was the first pushrod Norton to go back into production in 1946. In 1947, it gained Norton's famous 'Roadholder' front forks, yet retained a rigid rear end. The ES2, relaunched that year, had plunger rear suspension.

While Norton advertised on the basis of the company's racing heritage, in truth they were simply good, solid sporting singles. Many were used as sidecar tugs, still more, simply as basic transport. The Model 18 was also sold for trials use, but from 1949 to 1954 Norton offered a proper trials variant, the rigid 500T with a frame based on the wartime 16H.

A slow process of development followed and in 1953 the ES2 gained the swinging-arm frame used on the first Dominator twins. In 1954 the rigid Model 18 was phased out and the 600cc Model 19 was reintroduced. A 350cc Model 50, joined the range in 1956, and a new gearbox with a triangular selection mechanism was fitted to all the singles. In 1959, the Model 19 disappeared and the smaller variants found a new home – the revered Featherbed frame. After 1961, the singles gained the new Slimline frame, and this was the final chapter in their story. From then, Norton would concentrate on their twins range, while the 1965/66 ES2 Mk2 was nothing more than a cynically rebadged Matchless.

*Norton's 'long Roadholder' forks were fitted to the Model 18 from 1947. They offered good handling at the expense of a slightly heavy appearance at the front end.*

# BSA A10 Golden Flash

BSA's post-war parallel twins owed an obvious debt to Triumph's trend-setting Speed Twin of the 1930s, but in every detail the design was a true original. And in its own way, BSA was as influential as Triumph in making the layout such a staple of the British industry in the 1950s and into the 1960s.

There was a further link with Triumph, since some of the earliest design work on what would become BSA's twin was carried out by Val Page, the

*Solid, dependable and economical, the 650cc A10 twin shared a common heritage with Triumph's Speed Twin but had a character all of its own.*

engineer responsible for the Triumph parallel twin, the 650cc 6/1. More design studies were carried out by Edward Turner, designer of the Speed Twin, during some time spent at BSA in the war years. Most of the detail, however, was the work, of BSA chief designer Herbert Perkins, who had been with the company for many years. Near retirement age, he laid down the basis of the 500cc BSA A7, which was launched in 1946.

Among notable differences from the Triumph design were the use of a single camshaft with four lobes, carried behind the engine, instead of separate ones for exhaust and inlet.

Improvements and enhancements were made on both the A7 and A10, including sports versions with high-performance carburettors and tuned engines. The first major change came in 1954, with a new frame and swinging-arm rear suspension. This necessitated a change to the transmission. Alloy brake drums followed early in 1956, with a corresponding improvement in stopping power which was needed even more by the sports-tuned Road Rocket, introduced that year and good for 110mph.

The Golden Flash itself went on year by year, earning a reputation for dependability that endeared it to a generation of riders. As fashions changed, so BSA developed the unit engined A65 model, and the A10 was phased out in 1961, although the more sporting Super Rocket was to continue until 1963. That last year saw the introduction of the definitive sporting derivative, the Rocket Gold Star. This used a tuned 650cc sports engine in a Gold Star frame – a hybrid that worked so well that it overshadowed BSA's own replacement for the pre-unit 650cc twins. it was a fitting swan song for a much loved model.

*Plunger rear springing (above), a contemporary fad, offered only limited movement in comparison with rigid frames. Uneven chain tension could result in rapid chain wear.*

Some minor problems with the transmission and other features such as the lubrication were tackled in the ensuing years to make the A7 into a competent and reliable mount, though not one with a particularly high performance.

Much of the work involved in refining the design was carried out by Bert Hopwood. He soon had a further brief when news of Triumph's plans for a larger version

### BSA A10 Golden Flash

*Years in production:* 1950–61
*Engine type:* twin-cylinder overhead valve four-stroke
*Bore and stroke:* 70 x 84mm
*Capacity:* 646cc
*Compression ratio:* 6.5:1
*Power:* 35bhp @ 4500rpm
*Gearbox:* four-speed
*Weight:* 395lb (plunger)

*A handsome engine (below), bearing BSA's 'piled arms' badge on the timing cover, the iron-barrelled A10 power unit had many detail differences compared to the rival Triumph and Norton offerings.*

of their twin leaked out; BSA decided to follow suit, with a deadline of October 1949, the Earls Court Show. Starting in May 1949, the design work was carried out in around four weeks, and the model was in prototype form inside five months. The rush job proved to be worth it, as the A10 Golden Flash was a success from the start, with few problems. The Golden Flash name referred to the paint scheme, applied overall, although black and chrome was offered as an option. The new iron-barrelled engine gave a useful 35bhp and the then-new plunger suspension system added to rider comfort, although at the expense of handling as the plungers wore.

# Royal Enfield Bullet

Royal Enfield's much loved range of Bullet singles typify much of the best of British tradition. Unglamorous, but sturdy and reliable workhorses, they also possess the virtually unique distinction of having remained in volume production for a period approaching half a century.

The Bullet name, which harked back to Royal Enfield's association with gun manufacture, first appeared in the early 1930s. It was applied to a full range of 250, 350 and 500cc overhead-valve singles; lighter, tuned sports versions of the firm's existing models. But it was with the 350cc model that the name was most associated from the outset, and the Bullet range was particularly aimed at the sport of trials, which was then contested by modified road machines with little more special equipment than a high-level silencer.

With the start of the war, Royal Enfield became a major supplier of motorcycles to the armed forces, some 30,000 overhead-valve 350cc WD/CO, based

heavily on the pre-war trials machines. These formed the backbone of the first few years of the company's peacetime production, but in February 1948 the first post-war Bullet appeared.

Appropriately enough, the prototypes were entered in an important trial, where two first-class awards were gained. The Bullet was a pioneer of swinging-arm suspension. Although rear suspension was starting to gain favour for road use, it was much derided for trials, where the emphasis had always been on keeping the rear wheel in ground contact and relying on a slogging motor to carry the machine through. It was later on in 1948 that the Bullet really started to prove itself by winning the trophy at the International Six Days' Trial, the ISDT, where two riders also took gold medals, the only ones awarded to 350s.

## Royal Enfield Bullet (1952)

Years in production: 1948–96
Engine type: single-cylinder ohv four-stroke
Bore and stroke: 70 x 90mm
Capacity: 346cc
Compression ratio: 6.2:1
Power: 18bhp
Gearbox: Albion
Carburettors: 1in Amal
Tyres (front/rear): 3¼ x 19in

*The unmistakable shape of the Bullet engine (left) is visible in machines made four decades later in India, although more modern electrics have replaced the Magdyno behind the cylinder.*

The production models came onto the market the next year, and were broadly similar to the prototypes. Following a Royal Enfield convention, the engine appeared to be a wet-sump design, but actually used an oil tank cast as part of the crankcase. The gearbox, a four-speed Albion design, was bolted to the back of this, resulting in a compact and rigid unit as befitted its competition status. The new frame had a single front downtube and swinging-arm real suspension, as well as Enfield's own telescopic forks at the front. Both wheels had 6in brakes, and the rear wheel incorporated Enfield's cush-drive hub.

The new design was such a success that the competition version was soon joined by road bikes, while the trials and scrambles machines continued winning. The Bullets were developed over the ensuing years. A 500cc version appeared in 1953, alloy brakes were introduced, and a new styling feature, the cast-alloy Casquette, formed a combined steering head, instrument panel and light housing. There were a number of other variants before the Bullet range was dropped in 1962 – but not quite. While Royal Enfield themselves used the name on a number of later models, the rights to manufacture the original were sold to a company in India, where today it is still produced in a variety of versions. Eloquent testament to the soundness of the basic design.

*With its upswept silencer and swinging-arm frame, the compact Bullet hints at its original trials derivation.*

# Sunbeam S8

Designed as Britain's answer to the BMW, the Sunbeam S7 and later the S8 were odd mixtures of the inspired and the impractical, which was ultimately to condemn them to being an interesting backwater, rather than part of the mainstream of post-war motorcycling.

Several influences were at work, but the new machines were BSAs in all but name. Sunbeam had ceased to be a truly separate entity during the 1930s, and the trademarks now belonged to the giant BSA organisation, which reasoned that they could capitalise on Sunbeam's 'gentleman's motorcycle' image for their new tourer.

The design was the work of independent designer Erling Poppe, but was heavily based on the BMW R75, manufacturing rights to which had been offered to BSA as part of the war reparations. But while the double-cradle frame and telescopic fork echoed the BMW, the engine unit was a completely new design. Displacing 487cc, the engine was basically a parallel twin not unlike that offered by the BSA A7, but it was housed

## Sunbeam S8 (1952)

*Years in production:* 1946–56
*Engine type:* parallel twin (in-line) overhead-cam four-stroke
*Bore and stroke:* 70 x 63.5mm
*Capacity:* 487cc
*Power:* 24 bhp @ 6000rpm
*Carburettor:* Amal
*Tyres (front/rear):* 4¾ x 16in/ 4¾ x 16in
*Wheelbase:* 57in
*Weight:* 430lb (S7) 413lb (S8)

in alloy castings and turned around so that the crankshaft ran in line with the frame.

The first of the Sunbeam's problems arose from the choice of transmission. The intention was to use a shaft drive like the BMW, but the design adopted had a worm gear in place of the German machine's bevels. While easier to manufacture, it was inherently weak, and on prototypes the worm stripped its thread if the engine was fully used. The second problem was vibration. This had been evident on the prototypes, but the signs were ignored until the bike went into production in 1946. When an initial batch was despatched to a police team intended to escort King George VI, it was reported that they were unridable.

The machine weighed more than 400lb – but looked heavier. Fitted with 16in 'balloon' tyres, its handling was prone to vagueness, which became aggravated as the plunger rear suspension units wore. The finish, in BSA's rather drab 'Mist Green', can hardly have helped its showroom appeal, any more than the stories of its mechanical defects, and it was a poor seller.

In 1949 BSA decided to tackle both the performance and the styling by launching the new S8 as a sports alternative to the touring S7. Lighter than its predecessor, this used cycle parts such as forks and wheels from other BSA models. It was a more popular machine than the S7, but was still no runaway success. BSA finally discontinued the Sunbeams in 1956.

*Handsome and more conventional, the S8 answered many of the problems of the original S7, but it still suffered from the same mechanical weaknesses.*

# Vincent Black Prince

Phil Vincent was a great innovator. Having pioneered his own suspension design and created the fastest road vehicle of its time, in 1954 riders expected his latest Series D to be something special. Indeed it was, for Vincent offered a pioneering, fully enclosed aerodynamic motorcycle.

As events would prove, this was a serious miscalculation on his part, for the customers who had loved the brutal exposed engines of his earlier machines were left cold by the Series D styling. Technically it was superb, and offered a glimpse of the fully faired sports machines of the future. Press tests extolled its weather protection, economy and speed, but all-important sales were slow to follow. Meanwhile, the competition was becoming faster, better suspended and, above all, cheap.

Yet Vincent's logic was impeccable. All motorcycles were facing competition from lower-priced cars, at a time when both still represented alternative modes of transport rather than leisure accessories.

The Series D modifications were applied to the whole range: the Rapide, Black Shadow, Black Knight and range-leading Black Prince. Technical changes included coil ignition and engineering alterations. The chassis underwent major modification, the fabricated steel backbone that formed an oil tank was replaced by a simple tube, which proved weaker, and separate tank There was a new rear subframe/seat support and a hand lever to remove the chore of putting the bike on its stand. Problems with supply of glass-fibre meant that some Series D machines were supplied in naked form. Even so, many thought the appearance ugly.

Meanwhile another venture, the Amanda water scooter was causing Vincent difficulties. Predating the jet ski by a quarter of a century, its technical and safety problems, plus the discovery that Vincent was losing money on bike sales, pushed the company into closure. The last Vincent was built barely a week before Christmas 1955. It is a strange twist of fate that the enclosed models, through rarity, are now among the most sought-after of the survivors.

Under the skin, Vincent's mighty 1000cc 50 degree V-twin (left) was much as before.

## Vincent Black Prince (1955)

Years in production: 1954–55
Engine type: 50 degree V-twin ohv
    four-stroke
Bore and stroke: 84 x 90mm
Capacity: 998cc
Compression ratio: 7.3:1
Power: 55bhp @ 5700rpm
Carburettors: 1¹/₁₆in Amals
Tyres (front/rear): 3¹/₂ x 19in/
    4 x 18in
Weight: 460lb
Top speed: 120mph (est)

While the styling caused plenty of raised eyebrows, there was no denying the efficiency of the weatherproofing, or of the aerodynamics. The range-leading Black Prince had the practicality of a scooter with the performance of the mighty Black Shadow.

# Ariel Square Four

Ariel's Square Four always had a special place in motorcycling mythology. A four-cylinder machine when such a thing was almost impossibly exotic, it was also a 1000cc at a time when even 500 was considered big. From 1955, when Vincent closed, the Square Four was by far the largest British bike.

The Square Four started as an idea in 1928, when Edward Turner – later to become the head of Triumph – was a young hopeful, hawking sketches of a revolutionary machine around the motorcycle industry. The idea found a home at Ariel, then one of Britain's most important manufacturers.

*A handsome machine, the late 1000cc version of Ariel's long-lived range leader was positioned as luxury tourer rather than sports bike.*

What Turner had sketched was effectively a pair of across-the-frame parallel twins linked by a pair of gears. While there were theoretical problems with the linking gears, the beauty of the scheme was its incredible compactness and the fact that all the opposing forces could be balanced to result in a super-smooth engine.

*Four pipes typify the MkII post-war machine (right), while the large oil tank wrapping round the engine was introduced in 1956.*

The original prototype was a 500, so small and light that it could be fitted into the frame of the contemporary Ariel 250. Easy to start and smooth, it used an overhead-camshaft that contributed to an overheating weakness. A revised version was unveiled in 1930 creating a sensation. In 1932, a 600cc form was developed, replacing the 500cc.

The Square Four was fast and proved it in 1933 when Ben Bicker took a modified 500 to Brooklands. The machine just failed to become the first British 500 to achieve 100 miles in an hour. Despite lapping at over 110, every attempt failed due to the overheating bugbear. In 1937 the engine was completely redesigned. For the first time, a 1000cc version joined the 600, and as an option, rear springing devised by Frank Anstey was offered. This gave constant chain tension but little movement requiring frequent attention.

After the war only the larger version went back into production, now with a modern telescopic fork. However, it was heavier than it should have been, and in 1949 the engine became all-alloy, with coil ignition and a car-type distributor a year later. Acceleration, handling and cooling all improved.

The final development came in 1953, when the MkII version, sporting four separate exhaust pipes and numerous internal improvements, proved to be an excellent high-speed tourer.

However, the 'Squariel' was growing ever more expensive against the competition and the minor refinements introduced each year could not mask the fact that in some areas, such as cooling and rear suspension, it was not as refined as it could be. The last full production year was 1958, although the concept was developed as late as the 1970s by the Healey brothers completing around 20 specials – while Turner's linked crankshaft idea was employed to great effect by Kawasaki and others in racing.

## Ariel Square Four (1956)

*Years in production:* 1953–58 (4G Mk 11)
*Engine type:* four-cylinder ohv four-stroke
*Bore and stroke:* 65 x 75mm
*Capacity:* 997cc
*Compression ratio:* 6.45:1
*Power:* 42bhp @ 5800rpm
*Carburettor:* SU
*Weight:* 460lb
*Top speed:* 107mph

# Douglas Dragonfly

Against a background of financial uncertainty, the Douglas factory was always willing to rise to the challenge, pioneering innovative designs and styling. In 1954, they launched a sophisticated and original looking design at the Earls Court show.

Developed during 1953, the model was intended to supersede their rather dated range and take the company into a new era. Many of its features foreshadowed those of the slightly later BMW, which went on to achieve considerable success.

Douglas' new engine design was a 350 based on their previous engine – although it also borrowed heavily from an interesting 500cc prototype shown in 1951. The engine had been strengthened internally and cleaned up externally, with a streamlined appearance and a crankcase that housed the

electrics and other ancillaries, while the gearbox was attached to the rear. A single Amal Monobloc carburettor fed both cylinders. Coil ignition and alternator electrics were among the model's advanced features. Most of the cycle parts were bought in. The frame was completely new, made by the Reynolds Tube Company. A swinging arm with twin dampers looked after the rear suspension, while the front suspension used a design patented by Midlands engineer Ernie Earles and built by Reynolds. This used a long swinging arm, controlled by twin dampers. A similar design was used by BMW on their production bikes, while MV Agusta, among others, tried it for racing.

*A handsome machine with the styling of a miniature BMW, the Dragonfly's obvious charms were let down by a lack of power and the company's limited finances, which prevented it being fully developed.*

## Douglas Dragonfly (1956)

*Years in production:* 1953-56
*Engine type:* horizontally-opposed twin-cylinder four-stroke
*Bore and stroke:* 60.8 x 60mm
*Capacity:* 348cc
*Ignition:* Coil, with Miller alternator
*Carburettor:* Amal Monobloc
*Weight:* 365 lb
*Top speed:* 75mph

The other main styling feature was the petrol tank and light unit. Containing a massive 5 2 gallons, the tank pressing continued forward of the steering head to house the headlamp and instrument panel, which did not turn with the steering. Originally called the 'Dart', by the time of the show the model was called the 'Dragonfly'. Finished in a cream shade called 'light stone' with toning green panels or black-and-gold, it was an attractive if unconventional machine.

Unfortunately, after its much-vaunted show launch, Douglas was unable to offer quantity production for another nine months. Despite a favourable road test in April 1955, the price had gone up by almost 10 per cent by August, and a less favourable road test followed.

Its handling could not be faulted, although the brakes were rather poor. But ultimately the problem for the Dragonfly came down to a mismatch of its capacity and its presentation. With the styling and fittings of a tourer, it had an engine that was pushed to top 75mph and cruised at considerably less. It found few customers – only around 1500 were made – and Douglas' shaky finances restricted both manufacturing and marketing. Towards the end of 1956, the company was taken over by the Westinghouse electrical group, and motor-cycle production ended in March 1957.

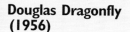

# Norton Dominator

Inspired by the popular success of Triumph's pre-war Speed Twin, and aware that other factories were working on their own versions, Norton realised that if they were to have any future after World War 2, they too needed a twin engine.

The job was undertaken by Bert Hopwood, who had worked on the development of Edward Turner's original Speed Twin design and had a vast experience in the industry. In 1947 Hopwood laid out his design, which aimed to improve on the Triumph's weaknesses, such as poor cooling, and incorporated some new ideas of his own. Chief among these was the use of only a single camshaft for inlet and exhaust valves, in place of the two used by Triumph and all the other factories.

The design had to work within the constraints of Norton's antiquated manufacturing machinery, as well as running on the poor quality post-war 'Pool' petrol. And for reasons of economy, it had to fit into the existing single cylinder model's frame. Such thoughts as these were behind the choice of a single carburettor, with close inlet ports and splayed exhausts.

Fitted into plunger cycle parts from the range-leading ES2 single, with some cosmetic changes including a special tank and mudguards, this became the Norton Model 7 Dominator, launched in 1949.

With a soft tuning, it offered little real challenge to Triumph's twin – but it could still reach 90mph and offered excellent reliability and handling in the Norton tradition. It was phased out in 1956, having long been overshadowed by its replacement, the De-Luxe, or Dominator 88, which first appeared in 1953. What made the 88 special was its frame, a close copy of the successful 'Featherbed' used on the works Manx Norton racers. Weighing some 40lb less than the Model 7, it handled and went rather better than its predecessor.

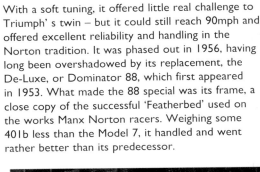

*Flat Norton handlebars contributed to a comfortable riding position (right) and the famous 'Roadholder' forks assisted in the secure handling.*

In 1956 the 88 Dominator's engine received the benefit of some serious performance development. The engine was resized by enlarging both bore and stroke to give a new capacity of 600cc. Its power output went up from 29 to 31 bhp and the new model was given a new name, the Dominator 99. With a hotter camshaft and higher compression ratio, plus new carburettor, the model's number roughly equated to its top speed. There were also frame refinements to match the performance.

The next important change was in 1961–62, when a new 49 bhp 650cc model was announced and both the 88 and 99 came out in SS (Super Sports) versions.

The 600s were soon discontinued and in 1964 the first of a series of 750 models, the Atlas, appeared.

### Norton Dominator

*Years in production:* 1956–62
(Dominator 99)
*Engine type:* parallel twin ohv
four-stroke
*Capacity:* 596cc
*Bore and stroke:* 68 x 82mm
*Compression ratio:* 7.4:1
*Power:* 31bhp @ 6500rpm
*Carburettors:* 1$\frac{1}{16}$in Amal 376
*Ignition:* coil
*Wheelbase:* 56$\frac{1}{2}$in
*Weight:* 395lb
*Top speed:* 101 mph

*With a 'slimline' version of Norton's famous Featherbed frame adding comfort, Norton's Dominator twin offered the best handling standard package available.*

# Velocette MSS

## Velocette MSS (1956)

*Years in production:* 1954–68
*Engine type:* ohv four-stroke single
*Bore and stroke:* 86 x 86mm
*Capacity:* 499cc
*Compression ratio:* 6.75:1
*Power:* 23 bhp @ 5000rpm
*Weight:* 375lb
*Top speed:* 80mph

The MSS first appeared in 1935 – a 500cc sports model designed to fit into the 'M' series comprising the 250 MOV and 350 MAC. As part of the series, it was an overhead-valve single with Velocette's own development of a high camshaft driven by intermediate gears, and short pushrods. These were designed to give the low reciprocating masses of an overhead-cam model and similar reliability, and succeeded – giving the MSS a speed not too far short of the company's race-derived 'K' models.

Velocette MACs were among a number of machines produced for military use, but only one MSS was tested by the army, and production ended for the duration. The 'M' series reappeared soon after the war, but as the factory were soon directing all their efforts into the 'revolutionary' pressed steel LE, all but the MAC were discontinued.

The MAC underwent a programme of development throughout the early 1950s. There were many detail changes to the engine, but the most important changes were to the chassis, with Velocette's own telescopic forks appearing in 1951 and a swinging-arm frame with Velocette's patented adjustable shock absorbers in 1953.

The year 1954 saw the relaunch of a model called the MSS, but in truth this was a very different proposition from pre-war days. The engine was of much shorter stroke, giving 'square' dimensions in its alloy barrel. The bottom end was similarly updated, and although the engine was softly tuned it was a modern design with considerable in-built strength. Despite the soft tune, the MSS was no slouch, being good for 80 mph or more, while the spring frame offered excellent handling.

It was no surprise, therefore, that it started to be tuned for higher performance. In 1955 a very rare scrambles version was offered, while 1956 launched the sports Venom model. This began a series in which higher and higher performance was achieved at the expense of the very flexibility and usability that had been the reason for introducing the pushrod models.

The underlying machine changed little, keeping outdated features such as the separate magneto long into the 1960s. It was such factors as the difficulty of obtaining supplies of components, coupled with the factory's increasing financial problems, that contributed to the end of the model in 1968. But its appeal lives on, with the qualities of the long-legged, economical single cylinder engine at the heart of the experience.

*Classic single: a pre-war finish and virtues were evident in a machine that was relaunched, albeit heavily redesigned, almost 20 years after it first appeared in the 1930s.*

# Norton International

In pre-war days, the Norton Model 30 had been the racing flagship of the range, but by World War 2 the pure racers had already begun to diverge from the publicly available International. When post-war production resumed in 1947, the 'Inter' had found a niche as a fast sporting roadster, and its single overhead-cam engine had become a vastly different proposition from the double overhead-cam racing Manx models.

The Inters achieved steady, though limited, sales for the next few years, and while some die-hard enthusiasts continued to race them in amateur competition, they were becoming dated against competition that included Triumph twins and the BSA Gold Star. Even so, several Clubman's TT winners of the late 1940s were mounted on Internationals fitted with special racing equipment, including an alloy cylinder barrel in place of the roadster's cast iron.

The final stage of development of the Inter came in 1953, when the alloy engine was installed in Norton's latest racing frame, the Featherbed, together with a new gearbox of the current design. In this form the International won its final Clubman's TT, although the Featherbed model was really intended as a sports special for fast road work.

The International's Featherbed frame was not quite a replica of the pure racers, but it was built to a higher standard than its roadster brothers. In any form, the Featherbed became the standard by which all handling would be judged for two decades, and with some of the best telescopic forks in the business, and braking to match, it could be pushed to the limit of its engine's considerable performance.

As a racing engine the 490cc overhead-cam unit although supremely rugged and reliable, was not very practical. It could be tricky to set up, with running clearances adjusted by numerous shims, and an oiling system that

relied on several hard-to-reach adjustable jets. The valves remained exposed resulting in incurable oil leaks. Roadster silencing stifled performance, and by the late 1950s it was possible to get the same level of power from a Norton Dominator.

### Norton Model 30

*Engine type:* single overhead cam single-cylinder four-stroke
*Bore and stroke:* 79 x 100mm
*Capacity:* 490cc
*Compression ratio:* 7.23:1
*Power:* 29.5bhp @ 5500rpm
*Carburettors:* 1⁵/₃₂in Amal TT
*Tyres (front/rear):* 3 x 19in/ 3¼ x 19in
*Wheelbase:* 55.5in
*Top speed:* 97mph

But such complaints missed the point. Full of class, sound and fury, the Inter both handled and braked superbly and allowed its lucky owner to believe that he was riding a real racer on the road.

The International was always expensive and by 1956 it was made to special order only. The last of the line left the works in 1958, when fewer than 20 were made. But the Inter had a pedigree borrowed from some of the most famous British racers, and a performance that kept riders enthralled for decades.

*Rider's eye view (right): Norton's straight handlebars and fork-top instrument panel were standard for the road-going Featherbed framed models.*

*Sharing the lines of the Manx racers, (below) the International used a similar Featherbed frame, but had an engine based on the single overhead-cam racing power unit.*

# BSA Gold Star

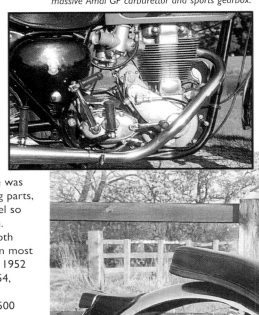

*The heart of it all : the all-alloy pushrod engine was developed from BSA's pre-war Empire Star, mated to a massive Amal GP carburettor and sports gearbox.*

Before the war, the BSA Gold Star had already become a legend. Post-war it went on to become the definitive sports single – unequalled in production racing and a force to be reckoned with in almost every form of motorcycle competition from trials to motocross.

The first post-war Goldie appeared at the 1948 Earls Court Show initially as a 350cc machine, its design included an alloy head and barrel that enclosed the pushrod tube. Most of the cycle parts were based on the touring B31, though new telescopic forks and a plunger rear suspension were added.

The top speed of the standard machine was much better than the B31, but on the low-octane fuel available was limited to less than 80mph. Fitted with the factory tuning parts, however, it could top 90mph. In 1949 a Clubman's model so equipped won the amateur 350cc race in the Isle of Man.

A 500cc version went on sale the next year, 1950. Both models gained a larger, 8in front drum brake and were in most respects identical. Detail improvements followed and by 1952 the 350 model could comfortably exceed 95mph. By 1954, after steady development, the 350 could top the 'ton' in Clubman's trim. What was the definitive version of the 500 appeared after 1955 and was given the DB type designation, this could top 110 mph with ease.

In 1956 the ultimate Goldie, the DBD34, was fitted with a host of race-proven tuning parts, including what was to become the legendary Gold Star silencer. On the over-run it produced a characteristic 'twitter' that was to become a well-loved feature. The cylinder head was revised to suit the largest sports carburettor available, the 1 1/2 Amal GP. The gearbox was given ultra-close ratios and its designation RRT2 became part of Gold Star mythology. The front brake was changed to an equally legendary Goldie component, the 190mm full-width alloy front drum. In Clubman's trim, the Goldie was fitted with the steeply angled clip-on handlebars, rearset footrests, swept-back exhaust, light alloy fuel tank and paired speedo/ rev counter.

*Clubman's cockpit (left): steeply angled handlebars, twin clocks, jutting headlamp on tubular brackets – the Goldie look helped to breed a generation of café racers.*

*The classic 1950s sports single – a BSA Gold Star DBD34 in the Clubman's trim, which included clip-on racing handlebars, rearset footrests, swept-back exhaust and 'twittering' Goldie silencer. Race-tuning extended to the close-ratio gearbox, which enabled a Gold Star to hit 50mph in first gear.*

## BSA Gold Star (1957)

**Years in production:** 1956–63 (DBD34)
**Engine type:** single-cylinder ohv four-stroke
**Capacity:** 496cc
**Bore and stroke:** 85 x 88mm
**Compression ratio:** 7.8:1
**Power:** 40bhp @ 7000rpm (42bhp with megaphone silencer)
**Carburettor:** 1½in Amal GP
**Tyres (front/rear):** 2¾ x 20in/ 3½ x 19in
**Wheelbase:** 56in
**Weight:** 305lb
**Top speed:** 110mph

The model so completely dominated the Isle of Man Clubman's TT that the series was redundant. After its first win in 1949 it won every year until 1956, when the series was discontinued. In that last victorious year, only two of the 350cc field rode anything else. In the 500 race, Gold Stars took all the first six places.

Perhaps the most versatile sports machine of all time, Goldies also won many top-class trials and scrambles throughout the 1950s.

With minor revisions, the customer Goldie continued until 1963 and was still being raced decades later.

# Triumph Tiger Cub

Triumph's Tiger Cub was designed unashamedly to appeal to admirers of the company's sporting twins. With the hand of master stylist Edward Turner in evidence, they were an attractive alternative to a string of lightweights powered by Villiers two-strokes. The 'Baby Bonnies' provided a desirable apprenticeship on two wheels for a generation of youths, and a ride-to-work bike with style. After 1960, when learners were restricted to bikes of less than 250cc, the Cub's appeal was enormously enhanced.

Although by the 1950s Triumph was very much associated with twins, thanks to its trend-setting Speed Twin and later derivatives, pre-war much of its production had centred on sports singles. The first post-war single was the much more mundane Terrier – a 150cc machine very much aimed at the commuter market, which Triumph had tended to forsake in recent years. Looking much like the Cub that followed, the Terrier was designed as a baby version of the twins, and was distinguished from many of its cheaper competitors by an air of completeness and quality. Its weakest points were rear suspension by plungers, and a big end assembly that proved rather too short-lived. The engine was built in unit with a four-speed gearbox and enclosed in a streamlined casing.

The first Cub, the T20, was simply a larger version of the Terrier, using the same plunger frame and cycle parts. A weak area of the frame that persisted for years was the swan-necked and unsupported headstock. This was braced by the tank, which was constructed in such a way that if this was replaced with another type of tank, the frame could prove extremely flimsy.

Apart from an increase in bore and stroke to give a capacity of 199cc, the engine unit changed little from original Terrier including its irritating drawbacks. It was particularly difficult to change the chain, and a new sprocket meant major dismantling, while the alternator caused electrical problems. The clutch and big end also had to be redesigned.

The Cub's bottom end was changed in 1956 to a plain bearing, but this also proved troublesome, especially in the hands of novice riders who would rev the engine before it had warmed up properly. Big end life in such circumstances was depressingly short, and Triumph suffered many warranty claims before this fundamental flaw was sorted out.

A competition (off-road) version called the T20C appeared in 1957, sporting a high-level exhaust and modified wheels and suspension. The basic styling remained that of the larger Triumphs.

There were numerous mechanical and styling changes over the years. Variations on a theme included sports and off-road versions, while in 1966 the Bantam Cub appeared – a hybrid with the baby Triumph engine in a BSA Bantam frame. The last Tiger Cub was the Super Cub, launched in 1967 and dropped a year later. But the Cubs had laid the seeds for its replacement by becoming the inspiration for the 250cc BSA C15, which appeared a decade later.

*Triumph's nacelle was a familiar styling feature. As well as rotary switchgear and the speedometer it incorporated a gear position indicator needle linked to the gearbox via a rock-and-pinion mechanism and cable.*

## Triumph Tiger Cub (1959)

*Years in production:* 1956–68 (all model variations)
*Engine type:* single-cylinder ohv four-stroke
*Capacity:* 199cc
*Power:* 14 bhp @ 6500rpm
*Carburettor:* Amal
*Tyres (front/rear):* 3¼ x 17in
*Weight:* 230lb
*Top speed:* 60mph

*Triumph's diminutive 200 provided an attractive alternative to a host of two-stroke lightweights. With styling borrowed from its bigger brothers, and a four-stroke single engine, it was the passport to two wheels for many a learner motorcyclist.*

# Panther M120

For many years the biggest single-cylinder machine in the world, Panther's 650 sloper announced that fact with a deep, lazy engine beat, which was said to 'fire every other lamppost'. With enormous torque and incredible economy, it was ideally suited to pulling the enormous sidecars that formed budget family transport.

The Model 120 was the final product of P&M of Cleckheaton, Yorkshire – the factory that had built its first motorcycle at the beginning of the 20th century with the revolutionary idea of using a sloping engine, instead of the front portion of a conventional frame. From first to last, it was this concept that defined Panthers, with gradual concessions to the engine and suspension designs of the changing years.

By the 1930s the form of the big single Panther had pretty much settled, and the firm also survived through the lean early years of the decade, thanks to the excellent volume sales of the ultra-cheap Red Panther 250cc lightweight which sold for under £30.

After the war the machines that appeared bore a close resemblance to the pre-war models. The Model 100 Panther for 1946 was a 600cc single with rigid frame and girder forks. it was ideal for economical sidecar use, with a fuel consumption in excess of 60 mpg.

In 1947 Dowty Oleomatic air-sprung telescopic forks were fitted – a form of front suspension that was very efficient when new, but gave problems when older as the seals wore. There were minor improvements to various parts of the bike until

*Handsome, solid and dependable, the 650cc Panther Model 120 was rarely seen in solo form; most performed sterling service as power for the family sidecar.*

1954 when a new, conventionally sprung fork and a swinging-arm frame were adopted. Styling changes followed, and the rigid model was discontinued in 1957.

The main news for 1958 was the development of the larger Model 120, closely based on the 600cc. But prototypes had engine problems, largely due to the increased stress and problems with Panther's unusual lubrication system. The production bikes were substantially improved, and offered lower fuel consumption – 70 mpg with a sidecar – than their predecessor. The Model 120 was ideally suited to sidecar use. In 1959 Panther's own sidecar chassis was an option – and this even included a towbar for a trailer.

## Panther Model 120

*Years in production:* 1959–66
*Engine type:* single-cylinder ohv four-stroke
*Capacity:* 649cc
*Bore and stroke:* 88 x 106mm
*Compression ratio:* 6.5:1
*Power:* 27bhp @ 4500rpm
*Gearbox:* Burman four-speed
*Tyres (front & rear):* 3½ x 19in
*Wheelbase:* 59in
*Turning circle:* 19ft 6in
*Weight:* 426lb

The simple, generally understressed big Panthers offered vintage values in a changing world. But sales of all Panther's range had been falling since the end of the 1950s, and by 1962 the firm was in receivership. An enlightened receiver kept them in production for a few years, mainly using up existing spares. But when difficulties arose obtaining major components – the separate Lucas Magdyno and Burman gear-box, which were by then virtually outmoded – there was no realistic way forward.

The last Panthers were built in 1966, although they remained on sale for at least a year after that. They were extremely cheap, but times had moved on and there was no longer any demand for the big sidecar outfit, as cheap cars took over that role and big bikes began the move towards becoming leisure vehicles.

*Slogging power (below): the long stroke sloper engine possesses a legendary torque, despite its antiquated layout. The forward projecting casting is an oil reservoir, part of a near-vintage lubrication system.*

Manufacturers' badges from 1940 to 1959

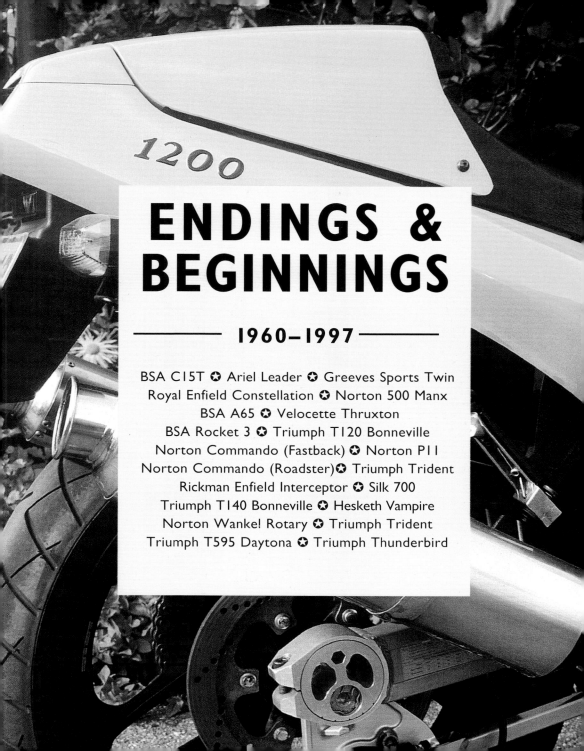

# ENDINGS & BEGINNINGS

## 1960–1997

BSA C15T ✪ Ariel Leader ✪ Greeves Sports Twin
Royal Enfield Constellation ✪ Norton 500 Manx
BSA A65 ✪ Velocette Thruxton
BSA Rocket 3 ✪ Triumph T120 Bonneville
Norton Commando (Fastback) ✪ Norton P11
Norton Commando (Roadster)✪ Triumph Trident
Rickman Enfield Interceptor ✪ Silk 700
Triumph T140 Bonneville ✪ Hesketh Vampire
Norton Wankel Rotary ✪ Triumph Trident
Triumph T595 Daytona ✪ Triumph Thunderbird

# Endings and Beginnings

As the 1960s dawned, they ushered in a new era in motorcycling — and a combination of powerful forces that would soon see the British industry reduced from a world leader to an also-ran, and finally to near-oblivion. And yet, during a decade that would see the creation of some of the best-loved British machines of all time, it was hard to spot where the downfall began. A third of a million new machines were registered in 1959 and everything seemed to be booming. It seemed as though there was plenty of room in the market place for everyone. Great names such as AJS, BSA, Matchless, Norton, Triumph and Velocette were still offering a wide range of singles and twins with traditional qualities of dependable economy and sporting performance. There were exciting new models such as the radical Ariel Leader/Arrow, and new twins from Norton, BSA and Triumph. Such smaller independent concerns as Cotton, Greeves and DMW offered a wide range of budget models with two-stroke engines, mostly from the long-established Villiers factory, with similar models from Francis Barnett or James.

The shadows on the horizon are easier to spot with hindsight. One was the introduction of the Mini. Costing around the same as a top-of-the-range motorcycle, it was the beginning of the end for bikes as basic transport. Another factor was the launch of the Honda Dream in 1959. Here was a 250cc that could run rings around many machines twice its size and had an electric-starter, to boot. Against this, the British industry was fielding machines powered by the low-powered Villiers two-strokes and the badly flawed Norton Jubilee pushrod twin. In 1961 Honda, Yamaha and Suzuki rapidly began to establish themselves as major forces in racing as well as roadsters.

Motorcycling itself was attracting a bad press, with scare stories in the papers about mods and rockers and a rising accident rate. The year 1960 saw the introduction of a limit on learners to machines of under 250cc, while insurance rates also started to creep up, discouraging young riders.

By this time, the British industry consisted mainly of the giant BSA-Triumph group and the lesser Associated Motorcycles (AMC) in South London.

*The 1963 film The Leather Boys (above) illustrated many of the problems which would come to bedevil the British bike industry over the next decade. Bikes were increasingly coming to be seen as a fringe pursuit with a questionable image, while the staple pushrod parallel twins were already looking dated compared to developments abroad.*

*Traditional factories such as the Ariel plant (below) of the 1950s, relied on labour-intensive hand building. But the BSA-Triumph group, which owned Ariel were alive to the need for change, installing new lines and computer controls at the BSA factory in Small Heath, which made the factory one of the most modern in the world.*

There were plenty of small independents, too, such as Royal Enfield or Velocette, although many of the great names, for example Vincent, had disappeared.

Whatever the cause of the British industry's troubles, it was certainly not just a lack of foresight. Both the major conglomerates had invested sums in development throughout the 1950s and on into the 1960s. AMC retooled extensively in the 1950s and BSA in the 1960s equipped its Small Heath plant with state-of-the-art computer controls.

Some of this investment was misguided, such as the setting up in 1967 of a group research and development facility at Umberslade Hall, a country estate near Solihull, equidistant from each of the main factories. Besides being very costly in itself the R&D staff were remote from production problems, while traditional factory rivalries still existed.

AMC had no such capital to invest and saw their traditional customer base being eroded by degrees. The group's proud road racing record was largely behind it, with the famed Manx Norton winning its last TT in 1961, while the privateer racers, the 350cc AJS 7R and 500cc Matchless G50, were phased out in the mid-60s. The days of the traditional big single were virtually over, and, despite a reputation for assembly and finish, the crunch came in 1966 against a background of falling sales. The Norton factory had

previously had to be closed in 1962 and moved to London. Such rationalisation was too little, too late, and the company was acquired by the industrial group Manganese Bronze Holdings. At a stroke, Francis Barnett and James were no more. From that time until the late 1960s, when Norton and Villiers amalgamated, only the bigger Nortons and Matchless models were made.

Many smaller factories were forced to close as a result of the Norton-Villiers merger, for Villiers was the last volume supplier of proprietary engines. Of the important small independents, only Greeves had developed sufficiently to manufacture their own engines, and such names as Cotton and Dot were forced to look overseas, or fold, which eventually happened.

Another great name had disappeared in 1963, coincidentally the first year of MOT tests for machines of over five years old. Ariel, as part of the BSA group moved from their Selly Oak factory to BSA's Small Heath plant, and ceased to be.

*Final fling: the Norton Commando and Triumph Bonneville was the ultimate development of an engine concept that could be traced back to before the war, although the innovative frame concept of the Commando in particular proved that there was still plenty of life in the old ideas.*

*The refusal of the workers at Triumph's old Meriden plant to accept redundancy culminated in a sit-in at the factory (left) and many months of unrest, after which new owners NVT were forced to accept defeat. Government funding helped the Meriden workers' cooperative to continue in production for several years in the late 1970s.*

*Great white hope (below): the Norton rotary was developed from one of the last projects of the old BSA research factory. Many years of development proved that the idea worked.*

The revamped Norton Villiers group started with the appointment of a new chief designer and developed a new model that would become a great name of the industry – the Commando.

Such new models were very necessary. The British industry's onetime confidence that the Japanese would confine themselves to small machines had been shattered by the arrival of the Honda 450 'Black Bomber' in 1965, and while this was never a bestseller, it paved the way for other larger machines from Japan. By this time, it was also well known that Honda was working on the epoch-making 750 Four.

BSA-Triumph were in serious trouble. Almost all their new developments had failed to bring them the hoped for benefits and many ageing models had been discontinued. However, in 1968 the group announced its new models, which were both to become legends. These were the Triumph Trident and BSA Rocket III – both derived, not so much from the group's new R&D headquarters, as a reworking of the forty-year-old Triumph Speed Twin. Still, they were great bikes and sorely needed.

Many of the major manufacturers' promising ideas had failed to make it into production. Of the smaller independents, Royal Enfield and Panther were already part of history, while Velocette was on its last set of wheels.

The launch of the first Japanese superbikes in 1969 hit the British bikes hard. Disastrous losses culminated in a rescue plan in 1972, which would merge BSA/Triumph with Norton Villiers to form Norton Villiers Triumph (NVT) in 1973.

*Great survivor (above): the Villiers-engined AJS Stormer, one of the last machines from the old AMC combine in the 1960s. Updated and still made by former development engineer Fluff Brown.*

The biggest side-effect of the merger came with the proposed reorganisation of the factories. This would have resulted in closure of the old Triumph plant at Meriden, Coventry, but the 1750 workers took exception to this and undertook a sit-in. After a year-and-a-half, during which NVT was unable to get access to the Trident parts held in the factory, the model had to be effectively discontinued. With falling sales of the Commando, NVT's Norton plant virtually gave up production after 1976.

The great survivor, somewhat perversely, was Meriden, where after a long-drawn-out struggle, the government finally stepped in with funding to start the Meriden Cooperative in 1975. They continued building what they knew best, Triumph twins, as well as continuing their own efforts to assemble machines from overseas parts.

Many smaller independents continued, including Hickman, Weslake, Seeley, Spondon and Silk. But such efforts were virtually doomed to remain small, for most of the British component suppliers were disappearing or diversifying.

This did not mean that there were not people prepared to try. In the late 1970s Lord Hesketh captured the public imagination with news of the latest British 'world-beater', designed to take on the best foreign competition. It was the sort of good news which the industry needed – in 1982, the Meriden Co-op folded, and the last remaining Bonnevilles were now being assembled in small numbers in Devon.

*A reborn Triumph has embraced the best of new technology (left), including robots, as well as traditional skills to enable it to compete for world markets at the highest level.*

Hesketh's efforts failed, and from this time on, the British bike was virtually a cottage industry. Although the burgeoning interest in older 'classics' helped to keep specialist frame-builders and skilled engineers in business.

The one obvious ray of hope during the 1980s was Norton, the inheritor of one of BSA's own 'world-beaters' using rotary engine technology. Sadly, it was too little, too late, and Norton all but disappeared in a welter of accusation and counter-accusation of financial mismanagement.

And so it all might have ended, except for Triumph. Virtually unnoticed for several years, and deliberately avoiding the kind of publicity that Norton and Hesketh had courted, the new owner of the remnants of the old Meriden assets had set out to make a range of machines which would genuinely merit the 'world-beater' tag. Accepting the new era of design and the new commercial realities of the late 1980s and 1990s, the reborn Triumph had almost nothing to do with the old, except the name and the loyalty which that could command. Triumph is proof that the skills that helped to make the British bike the envy of the world still exist. As all those behind the mergers and start-ups of the last 20 years of the industry had hoped, it is simply a matter of providing the proper environment in which those skills can be expressed.

*Modern volume production depends on components that are either made in-house, sourced overseas or from a handful of specialist suppliers, as many of the biggest names in British motorcycle components are no longer in business.*

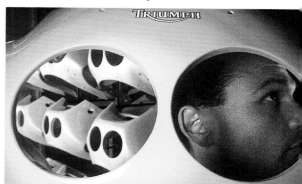

# BSA C15T

BSA's lightweight singles of the 1960s symptomised much of what was wrong with the British industry at the time. Yet they provided transport for thousands of young riders, and the trials versions helped usher in the modern era of off-road sport, while being very successful in their own right.

BSA had acquired the Triumph marque at the start of the 1950s, and the lightweights towards the end of the decade owed far more to Triumph than to BSA. Chief among them was the 1958 C15 Star. A 250cc fourstroke almost totally derived from the 200cc Triumph Tiger Cub. Even so, the new model seemed both up-to-date and sophisticated, with its light weight and sophisticated electrics. As with its Triumph predecessors, the C15 and its derivatives suffered from minor electrical problems, oil leaks and somewhat complicated maintenance routines. But it went well enough and was mainly reliable. The SS80 sports version, which appeared in 1961, was faster, while the 350 version, the B40, offered more power. In the mid 1960s a similar engine layout was seen in the 75cc Beagle and 50cc Ariel Pixie, two fatally flawed attempts by the BSA Group to launch an ultra-lightweight.

Over the years there were countless variations on the same theme, including sports and off-road versions, while the basic engine was stretched to 441 and finally 499cc. The engine even found its way back to Triumph, to power the street-scrambler-styled singles of the late 1960s . The last of BSA's C15 derivatives was the B50, built until 1973. Even after this, the specialist company CCM of Bolton built their own derivative of the B50 for off-road competition throughout the 1970s.

Off-road sport was long a speciality of BSA. In the post-war era, the 350 and 500 Gold Stars

Despite serious competition aspirations, the 250 still carried full road equipment (left) including electrics by the unreliable and unloved energy-transfer system.

Superficially the same unit as the roadster, the trials bike's all alloy engine (left) concealed a host of modifications, as well as a set of gearbox ratios more suited to off-road use. The iron-barrelled engine was derived from Triumph's Terrier and Tiger Cub, and itself spawned a whole generation of derivatives.

Relatively lightweight, with taut handling and good suspension, BSA's C15T capitalised on the virtues of the roadster to produce a trials bike that helped to usher in the modern era.

had been enormously successful trials and scrambles mounts, but the company correctly anticipated the shift towards lighter, more manageable machines. The lightweight, unit-construction C15 offered a great deal of potential, and the competition shop soon developed successful works specials ridden by expert rider and BSA employee Brian Martin.

Production versions followed the C15S scrambler and C15T trials machine. Superficially similar to the roadsters, there were in fact numerous differences, which included frames, wheels and suspension, as well as a host of engine and gear modifications.

The competition bikes succeeded famously. On the 441cc derivative, Jeff Smith won the world motocross championship in 1964 and 1965. It was the design's finest hour.

## BSA C15T (1960)

*Years in production: 1958–73 ,*
  *(C15T 1959–65)*
*Engine type: single-cylinder ohv*
  *four-stroke*
*Bore and stroke: 67 x 70mm*
*Capacity: 247cc*
*Compression ratio: 7:1*
*Power: 15bhp @ 5000rpm*
*Carburettor: Amal Monobloc*
*Exhaust: high level*
*Weight: 275lb*
*Top speed: 75mph*

# Ariel Leader

**Ariel Leader (1961)**

*Years in production:* 1958–65
*Engine type:* parallel twin
  two-stroke
*Bore and stroke:* 54 x 54mm
  (48.5 x 54mm)
*Capacity:* 249cc (199.5cc)
*Power:* 17.5bhp @ 6750rpm
*Carburettor:* Amal Monobloc
*Tyres (front & rear):* 3¼ x 16in
*Top speed:* 73mph

One of the most technically innovative offerings of the post-war years of the British industry, Ariel's futuristic two-stroke was designed for mass transport. As part of the giant BSA group, Ariel had been manufacturing its traditional four-stroke singles, the Square Four, and a version of the BSA 650 twin when, in 1955, BSA decided to turn the entire resource of the factory over to a revolutionary new design offering low maintenance and full weather protection.

They may have been influenced by the enormous boom in scooter sales, although the machine that was eventually produced was far from a traditional scooter. Instead, it was a full-size 250cc motorcycle, albeit with small (16in) wheels. It was built entirely of pressed steel, which was ideal for mass production, and offered tremendous strength. However, the initial cost of the tooling was high and expensive to modify.

Not that there was anything wrong with the final design which embodied sound logical thinking. It was based on a strong box beam that contributed to the excellent handling, and which, by acting as a low-slung fuel reservoir, helped to keep the centre of gravity down. The trailing-link forks with dampers concealed inside the legs worked extremely efficiently despite their odd appearance.

The engine hung below the main beam, and was designed as an integrated unit. A 250cc parallel twin with 180 degree firing interval, the cylinders were angled at 45 degrees to help keep the weight low slung.

When the Leader appeared in 1958 it offered an integral fairing and windscreen, and a dummy 'petrol tank' that was actually a luggage compartment, plus a host of practical and decorative extras. But many traditional motorcycle customers were not impressed by its styling while others were being attracted by the revolutionary Mini.

Its cost may also have been too high, and in an attempt to appeal to the more sporting customer, as well as offer a cheaper alternative, the Leader was redesigned as the unfaired Arrow, launched in 1960. Again, the styling was odd, but the machine was light with a decent performance, and it was much cheaper.

Ariel's entire production was devoted to the new range, and in a good month well over 1000 were produced. Tuning experiments upped the power of a works-developed model enough for it to come seventh in the lightweight TT, and the position looked promising.

For 1961 a new cylinder head improved the power of the standard machines, and a super sports version, the Golden Arrow, was also launched. But it proved unreliable. Starting could be poor, the gear change was rough, and some maintenance jobs were tricky. Two stroke technology of the time also meant that while the engine was quick. it was often smoky.

The construction of the beam frame, complete with dummy tank, is clear to see in the unfaired Arrow (above).

In 1963 the Ariel factory was absorbed into the main BSA plant. With cleaner, more practical machines appearing from Japan, the launch in 1964 of a 200cc version proved unsuccessful. Production ended in 1965, and with it the Ariel name, although it was resurrected by BSA for two spectacularly unsuccessful lightweights, the Pixie and the Ariel 3, over the next few years.

The fully enclosed Ariel Leader was introduced to fill a need for mass transport. Modern features included integral fairing and screen, optional panniers, indicators and many accessories.

# Greeves Sports Twin

Built by one of Britain's smallest manufacturers, Greeves lightweights were true individuals with an all-round quality that often put to shame the major motorcycle factories. The company took its name from Bert Greeves, but the business was run as a partnership with his cousin Preston Derry Cobb and started shortly after World War 2. In those early days the product was a motorised invalid carriage, and the company was called Invacar.

The invalid carriages sold well and established a firm foundation for the factory, based in Essex. The factory possessed its own foundry and very soon became expert in the new technology of fibreglass moulding. The invalid cars featured some innovative designs, notably suspension by rubber bushes that acted as self-damping springs when twisted.

By the early 1950s Bert Greeves, an enthusiastic motorcyclist and no mean off-road rider, was able to indulge his interests by constructing a prototype motocross machine. Production versions of both an off-road machine and a roadster appeared in 1954. Using Villiers or British Anzani engines, and suspension based on the invalid cars' rubber units, the frames illustrated another Greeves innovation. In place of the normal tubular front section and steering head was a single enormously strong aluminium alloy H-section beam.

It was the frame and front forks, that really set Greeves apart from the rest. Despite their strange appearance, they offered superb handling on or off the road. For a time there was public resistance to the design, but when experienced competition rider Brian Stonebridge joined the company in the mid 1950s, Greeves started to make a name for itself with an incredible series of giant-killing demonstrations, which vindicated their ideas.

Roadster production centred on a range of modest 250 and 325cc lightweight twins. By the 1960s the Sports Twins had become probably the best of their kind, thanks to Greeves handling and quality build. An indication of the regard in which they were held was their adoption as police bikes.

## Greeves Sports Twin (1961)

*Years in production:* 1956–63
   (with engine variations)
*Engine type:* 180 degree
   parallel twin two-stroke
*Bore and stroke:* 57 x 63.5
*Capacity:* 324cc
*Compression ratio:* 8.7:1
*Power:* 17bhp @ 5250rpm
*Carburettor:* Villiers 25mm
*Tyres (front/rear):* 20in/18in
*Weight:* 270lb
*Top speed:* 74mph

Numbers were small, however, with only around 300 racers and a few thousand roadsters appearing throughout the 1960s. Then Greeves began to fall victim to a number of pressures. First its engine supplier Villiers was taken over, and then the British market saw the influx of Japanese lightweights. Invacar, too, fell victim to the changing times. It was taken over in 1973, but in any case government support for specialist invalid cars ceased shortly after. The last Greeves roadsters had left the factory in 1968, but they had designed a new motocrosser around their own single cylinder 360cc engine. Its derivatives stayed in production until 1978, although a disastrous factory fire in 1976 was really the end of Greeves as a volume manufacturer.

*Competition machines (above) ran in parallel with the roadsters. Typical of the breed was this 246cc Model 24MDS scrambler, modified to take part in the 1963 ISDT.*

*With the company's distinctive alloy front-beam frame and forks, and a finish in Moorland Blue, the Sports Twin in either 250 or 325cc form was one of Greeves' best loved roadsters. Despite its reliance on proprietary engine, electrics and brakes, it offered superb handling and comfort.*

# Royal Enfield Constellation

Big parallel twins may have been the staple fare of the British industry in the late 1950s and 60s, but there were plenty of variations on the theme. With a character all its own, Royal Enfield's twin offered one of several alternatives to BSA/Triumph conformity, and was for several years the largest of its kind.

Royal Enfield's first post-war twin appeared in 1948 and owed more to the company's singles than the competition. A 500cc engine in the 350 single's swinging-arm frame, it featured separate heads and barrels that improved cooling and serviceability at some cost to strength, while the crankcase had a cast-in oil container at the rear. Ignition was by

battery, coil and distributor, and although the Albion gearbox was a separate unit. It was rather unimaginatively called the 500 Twin. A few years later the 1953 700cc Meteor went one better than the rival 650s by offering what was effectively a doubled-up 350 single. Design changes to the engine, lubrication system and cycle parts resulted in the 1956 Super Meteor. A year later, with the Vincent V-twin already gone, the big Enfield was the largest capacity twin on the market.

The 700cc Constellation launched in the USA in 1957, first appeared in Britain in 1958, along with a new, much lighter 500, the Meteor Minor. With new engine castings, the 'Connie' was sportier with a very robust bottom end, hot cams and, initially, a single racing Amal TT carburettor.

## Royal Enfield Constellation

*Years in production:* 1958–63
*Engine type:* 360 degree parallel twin ohv four-stroke
*Bore and stroke:* 70 x 90mm
*Capacity:* 692cc
*Compression ratio:* 8:1
*Power:* 51bhp @ 6250rpm
*Carburettor:* twin Amal Monoblocs
*Tyres (front/rear):* 3¼ x 18in / 3½ x 17in
*Weight:* 403lb
*Top speed:* 116mph

*Another classic Royal Enfield feature, the cast-alloy casquette (below) combined instrument housing, top yoke and light shell in one unit.*

*Beefy, purposeful and powerful, in its day the 'Connie' was the biggest British twin.*

With a suitably tuned cylinder head, the resulting bike was a real road-burner capable of well over 110mph. On test, it bettered 115mph. The racing carb disappeared in favour of twin Monoblocs in 1959, but the bike was still fast – although it soon gained a reputation for fragility, while the front brake was inadequate for the power and speed. In fact, there were a number of niggles, which meant that the model never achieved the popularity of the Triumph twins, despite its theoretical advantages and better acceleration.

To counter complaints of heavy vibration, the crankshaft was re-designed. The rather weak clutch was altered in 1961, and there were a number of styling changes. This became the ultimate example of the 'Connie', because in 1963, Enfield launched the even larger 750 Interceptor (actually a 736cc design) while the Constellation was relegated to sidecar duty before production ceased that year. The 750 twins only lasted a few years more before bowing out at the start of the 1970s, with the company suffering from the financial malaise of much of the industry.

# Norton 500 Manx

As a company, Norton was dominated by the demands of racing, and for many years a wide gulf separated their bread-and-butter products from the exotics developed in the race shop. While the policy might not have been ideal commercially, it produced one of the most phenomenally effective racers of all time – the Manx Norton single.

The Manx was itself a development from the single overhead-cam International racers.

*Finning that completely enclosed the bevel drive shaft (left) characteristic of the later, short-stroke models. The crankcase in Elektron magnesium alloy extends right up to the bottom fins.*

A dohc layout had been tried as early as 1937, with a larger cambox in which a gear train operated twin camshafts bearing directly on a pair of valve 'pushers' in contact with the valve stems. Inspired partly by experiments at rivals Velocette, this design was not immediately successful, although it reappeared in 1938 with revised engine dimensions and supposedly phenomenal power.

The Manx name was first used late in 1939, but in 1940 all racing efforts ceased. The name reappeared in 1946 before the amateur Manx Grand Prix, where several entrants rode that season's new racer. With an engine based on the pre-war International, the dohc cambox was used, while the machines sported the new telescopic front forks tried on the works bikes in 1938. Performance, however, was disappointing.

Gradually, steady process development began to pay dividends. In 1948 a twin leading-shoe brake appeared, and with 112mph potential, it was needed. By 1950, with 120mph performance, it was essential. The year 1950 saw a significant leap in Manx technology, with the adoption of the new 'Featherbed' frame. The new frame was a quantum leap for motorcycling, and gave Norton a massive edge over the competition. Its name was coined by rider Harold Daniell, enthusing about its comfort. After a triumphant debut in the hands of Geoff Duke in April, the Featherbed Nortons went on to win a double

hat trick at the TT, the first of many major wins. In 1951 both the 500 and 350 were listed as production racers – virtually identical to the works machines, the only significant differences being the engine size.

In 1953, the engines were redesigned with a much shorter stroke for improved revs, and more wins ensued, despite the sophistication of the mainly Italian multi-cylinder competition. In 1954 streamlining was tested, resulting in yet more wins, but it was becoming clear that time was running out for the antiquated technology. Norton 'officially' withdrew from Grand Prix racing at the end of the season, although they continued to support works entries, and rivals Moto Guzzi continued to race single cylinders with considerable success until 1957.

The factory continued to develop the Manx, and gained many more wins, while the production models continued in privateer competition for many years. Then, in 1961, Norton scored an amazing double hat-trick at the TT. It was effectively the model's swan song, although private enthusiasts developed and raced them for many more years.

The last batch appeared in 1962, the year in which the Norton works in Birmingham closed, and the factory moved in with AMC in Plumstead, London.

## Norton 500 Manx (1962)

*Years in production:*
  1946–53 (long-stroke)
  1953–62 (short-stroke)
*Engine type:* double overhead-cam
  single-cylinder four-stroke
*Bore and stroke:* 79.6 x 100mm
  (1946-53), 86 x 85.6 (1953-62)
*Capacity:* 499cc
*Compression ratio:* 9.75:1
*Power:* 50bhp @ 7200rpm
*Carburettor:* 1½in Amal GP
*Tyres (front/rear):* 3 x 19in / 3½ x 19in
*Wheelbase:* 56in
*Top speed:* 150mph (depending
  on gearing)

*Light, purposeful and developed to the pitch of sophistication, the late Manx Norton epitomises the British racing single at its best.*

# BSA A65

Along with its 500cc cousin, the A50, the problems that beset the A65 typify much of what went wrong with BSA towards the end of the company. The machines had a poor reputation for reliability and spares back-up in particular which helped to put the final nails in the coffin of a large part of the British industry. And yet the design had its good points, for with modification the engine unit proved itself in that most demanding of competitions – sidecar racing – while surviving, hard-working bikes have clocked up thousands of trouble-free miles.

By the 1960s BSA had become part of a large conglomerate with diverse interests. There had been a concerted effort to introduce new systems, and there was an on-going drive to attract sales in the American market. Despite the popularity of the existing 650cc twins, they were perceived as being antiquated and were losing out against Triumph.

The new models were developed quickly, and many of their problems were the kind that a longer testing period would have ironed out. On the face of it, though, the new 650 offered promise, being more sophisticated and lighter than its A10-based predecessors.

A unit-construction design with fashionable 'power egg' streamlined styling was coupled with a single, almost square, carburettor which promised a free-revving engine. It was perhaps surprising, therefore, that it initially offered less power than the top-of-the-range A10-based machine, the Rocket Gold Star. The frame and forks, were similar to the duplex cradle unit of the late A10s, and the handling was generally quite good, although the rather crude damping of the front forks found the going tough.

When the A65 and smaller A50 were launched in 1962, they appeared to have plenty going for them. The styling was in line with the clean, rather lumpy BSA look of the period. The performance was not bad, with strong acceleration and 100mph top speed – and the fuel economy was good.

The problems soon appeared, however. The engines were prone to vibration, and the main bearings self-destructed at low mileages, often wrecking the engine. Oil leaks were common and the primary drive chain was also prone to wear.

This did not prevent an A50 from taking Gold in the 1962 ISDT, while for the public, the A65 was soon offered in higher performance versions with sportier styling, higher and higher compression ratios, and latterly, twin carburettors. One such machine, the 650 Lightning, even managed to win a production race in 1965. For the all-important American market initially, there were many more variants, including scramblers.

*'Power-egg' styling was a popular fashion in the 1960s, and the 650 BSA unit was perhaps the definitive version. All functions in the unit engine were smoothly faired in behind streamlined alloy casings.*

## BSA A65 (1966)

*Years in production:* 1962–72 (all A65 variants) 1966-68 (Spitfire models)
*Engine type:* twin-cylinder ohv four-stroke
*Bore and stroke:* 75 x 74mm
*Capacity:* 654cc
*Compression ratio:* 10.5 : 1 (Spitfire MkII)
*Power:* 54bhp @ 4500rpm (Spitfire MkII)
*Gearbox:* four-speed
*Weight:* 383lb (Spitfire MkII)

By 1966 the top of the range was the Spitfire MkII, which sported many racing fittings, such as close-ratio gears, a larger front brake and fibre-glass tank. It was light and fast, with 120 mph within reach, and thanks to a new front fork, handled well. The introduction of 12v electrics was an improvement that benefited the whole range. But the vibration problems were still there and although attempts were made to find a cure, none succeeded. From 1970 on, this flawed power unit was coupled with a problematic frame. The oil-in-frame unit had a large diameter backbone which doubled as the oil tank. A similar design was adopted by Triumph, and although both handled well, the actual seat height precluded them being ridden comfortably by any-one much under six feet tall.

*Handsome in a beefy way, the A65 offered true sports bike performance and the handling to exploit it*

The model soldiered on until 1972, despite BSA's growing financial difficulties. By this time the seat height had been reduced to a much more workable level, handling was excellent and even the vibration seemed to have decreased. Sadly it was too late, and the A65 became a victim of BSA cuts.

A postscript to the story is that a solution to the main-bearing problem had been proposed while developing the factory racers in 1966–7, but never adopted. After the model had been discontinued, ex-BSA workers offered this as an after-market conversion, consisting of a new set of main bearings an optional new oil pump and clutch modification.

# Velocette Thruxton

The Thruxton Velo was the final development of Velocette's pushrod single – a machine that in essence dated back to the mid 1930s, but could top 110 and still sip fuel at an astonishingly low rate through its massive racing carburettor.

Thruxton is a race track in Hampshire – one of the many wartime airfields that found a new use during the 1950s. Racing centred on the endurance marathon for production machines, the 500-miler. The bikes were substantially catalogue models and

the entries were shared between two riders. Over the years many British stars shone in the event, including Dave Croxford and Percy Tait. Machines included the racing Triumph Bonneville, the John Player Norton Commandos – and the Velocette.

Velocette singles evolved slowly over the years. Their basic formula was laid down by the 1934 250cc MOV, with the camshaft mounted high up and the pushrods kept as short as possible, while their narrow crankcase, slimline clutch and out-

board chain run dated back to the early vintage days. By the late 1950s the machine had evolved into the 350cc Viper and 500cc Venom which went on to set the 24-hour speed record at an average of 100 mph-plus – an enduring record.

In 1964 the high-cam Velo reached its ultimate development. The performance of the Clubman's

*The ultimate sports pushrod engine (right): tuning the Thruxton included a special head with extra large valves and a down draught inlet port. This was matched to an enormous Amal GP carburettor that required special cut-aways in the tanks.*

Venom at Thruxton led to the makers offering a performance kit that included a special head with 2in inlet valve and an enormous Amal Grand Prix carburettor, plus oil and petrol tanks cut away. Although the 1965 500-miler was on an alternative circuit, the Velocettes dominated the race, with Dave Dixon and Joe Dunphy . The model soon found favour with sporting riders, for it was a genuine tuned roadster and was well able to cope with everyday use.

Its finest moment came in 1967 the year of the first Isle of Man Production TT. In the 500 class, Neil Kelly took the race at just under 90mph, as well as the fastest lap at over 91 mph. Fellow rider Keith Heckles was second.

Only a little more than 1200 Thruxtons were built, although the relative ease of converting a Venom meant that there were several more replicas constructed by private owners.

In 1969 the ignition system was modified to coil ignition, as the traditional magneto had been phased out by Lucas. This was effectively the swan song, for it bowed to commercial pressure in 1971, still a genuine family firm after 66 years.

*Production racer: (left) in 1967 the Thruxton dominated the inaugural Production TT, taking first, second and fastest lap. It was capable of more than 110mph and had proven endurance, having broken the 24-hour record.*

## Velocette Venom Thruxton

*Years in production:* 1965–71
*Engine type:* high-camshaft ohv
    four-stroke single
*Capacity:* 499cc
*Bore and stroke:* 86 x 86mm
*Compression ratio:* 9.2:1
*Power:* 41–47bhp @ 6200rpm
*Carburettors:* Amal GP
*Tyres (front/rear):* 3 x 19in/ 3¼ x 19in
*Wheelbase:* 54¾in
*Top speed:* 110 mph

# BSA Rocket 3

The late 1960s ushered in the age of superbikes – machines with specifications and performances much superior to anything that had gone before. Although the bikes that gave form to the name were Japanese, both BSA's and Triumph's triples were among the most important of the pioneers.

As part of the same manufacturing group, the BSA Rocket 3 and the slightly later Triumph Trident were based on the same original concept which dated back to the early 1960s. Designers Bert Hopwood and Doug Hele realised that it would be quite simple to graft an extra cylinder on to the 500cc Triumph twin, producing a 750cc three-cylinder engine. However, nothing was done with the idea for several years, until the company's board members were told of Honda's plans for a 750cc four-cylinder machine and a prototype was hastily put together. To save time, the cylinder blocks were made from cast iron, while the special sand-cast crankcase components also added weight. One clever feature of the design was the way in which the crankshaft was forged in one plane then heated and twisted to the correct angles.

*Science-fiction styling and superbike performance were the two main attributes of the 1968 BSA Rocket 3, designed to appeal to a largely American market.*

**BSA Rocket 3 (1968)**

*Years in production:* 1968–72
*Engine type:* three-cylinder ohv four-stroke
*Bore and stroke:* 67 × 70mm
*Capacity:* 740cc
*Compression ratio:* 9.5:1
*Power:* 60bhp @ 7250rpm
*Gearbox:* four-speed in unit
*Tyres (front/rear):* 3¼ × 19in/ 4 × 19in
*Wheelbase:* 57in
*Weight:* 490lb
*Top speed:* 120mph

*The crankcase (below) consists of separate castings bolted together, requiring care in assembly. Three exhausts lead into two pipes, terminating in the extraordinary 'ray gun' silencers with three short exit pipes.*

Two versions – BSA and Triumph – were actually developed, using a different engine and frame layout, with the BSA's engine angled forward in a duplex cradle frame. The crankcase was a bolt-up assembly of five major castings. Care in component selection and engine building were essential.

Production of the first Rocket 3 began in 1968, and the machine was launched in Britain early in 1969 – ahead of Honda's revolutionary 750 four. Road tests showed it was the fastest multi-cylinder machine of the era, and although it had slower acceleration than either the Norton Commando or the Honda, it had the legs of both at the top end.

In 1971, a Rocket 3 won the Daytona 200 in the United States, with a new race record speed, while a Trident placed second and another BSA was placed in third.

The styling was far less well-received. Designed by committee, and in response to the demands of the huge American market, the Rocket 3's slab-sided petrol tank, huge badges and 'ray gun' silencers were not what the traditional BSA buyer expected. Only about 7000 bikes were built before financial difficulties meant production shut down in 1972, leaving the Triumph Trident to inherit the mantle of the triples.

# Triumph T120 Bonneville

Triumph's Speed Twin had been one of the bikes that helped to set the pace before the war. After the conflict, the 500cc Speed Twin spawned many descendants, from 350 to 750cc capacity. Above all others, the 650cc Bonneville became the bike that set the standard throughout the late 1950s and 1960s – the era of the Rockers and Café Racers.

The first 650cc Triumph appeared in 1949, when the softly tuned 6T Thunderbird showed its pace at the Monthléry speed bowl before going on sale the next year. The model was an excellent tourer.

In 1951, a Thunderbird racer, equipped with twin carburettors, hot cams and high-compression pistons, reached 132mph at Utah's Bonneville Salt Flats. A few years later, in 1956, Johnny Allen achieved 214.4mph, a record accepted by the US authorities, but the world governing body refused to acknowledge it. Americans continued their efforts, and two years later a specially prepared Tiger 110 managed to achieve over 147mph, ridden by Bill Johnson. The speed was good enough for a class record. That was in 1958, and the venue once again was Bonneville.

The first Triumph machine to bear the Bonneville name appeared in 1959. Based heavily on

the Tiger 110, the T120 was fitted with the twin carburettors, together with the hot E3134 inlet cam. With a power rated at 46 bhp, the model was already good for a comfortable 115mph – but the engine had the potential to be tuned a lot hotter.

From 1963 they gained a new frame, with extra bracing for the swinging arm and steering head and a new compact power unit. The steering angle was changed and improved forks were adopted.

*Light and sporty, Triumph's 650 twin had an edge over its competitors, which made it the machine that a generation aspired to. Although its general layout harked back some 30 years.*

*Front braking (left) is by a twin-leading-shoe 8in diameter drum that stopped the light (370lb) package reasonably effectively.*

All these improvements helped the Bonneville to match its rivals' all-round performance. In the styling stakes, however, it had no equal. Where the contemporary BSA was worthy but perhaps a little stolid, and Norton's offering lacked the absolute glamour of its racing forebears, the 650 Bonneville oozed get-up-and-go.

On the race track, it got up and went! In 1967 and 1969 it won Production TTs and British 500 mile races. In 1969 the works TI00R achieved a 1/2/3 in the Thruxton 500-miler, covering three more of the top seven places.

In the opinion of many, the 1968 Bonneville is the best of the breed. With good handling and more reliable electrics than its predecessors (including a new ignition), all the good features were there in a package that was hard to beat.

But it was almost the end of the line. The 650 twin would only survive a scant three years before it was replaced by a new 750cc and Triumph began its slow slide into oblivion.

## Triumph T120 Bonneville

*Years in production:* 1959–71
*Engine type:* twin-cylinder ohv four-stroke
*Bore and stroke:* 71 x 82mm
*Capacity:* 649cc
*Compression ratio:* 8.5:1
*Power:* 46bhp @ 6700rpm
*Carburettors:* two 1³/₁₆in Amal Monoblocs
*Gearbox:* four-speed
*Wheelbase:* 55in
*Weight:* 370lb

# Norton Commando (Fastback)

Launched to rapturous acclaim at the Earls Court Show in 1967, and four times voted Machine of the Year, the Norton Commando was the best-loved product of the final years of the British industry. And yet it grew from a classic compromise. By the mid-60s, Associated Motorcycles (AMC), Norton's parent company, was in trouble. In late 1966 AMC was taken over by Manganese Bronze Holdings, a conglomerate which already owned Villiers. The motorcycle interests were amalgamated into one company – Norton Villiers.

Virtually all the current product consisted of 650 and 750cc Norton twins, using either the ageing Featherbed or Matchless frame. It was clear that the new company needed a flagship – and quickly, preferably by the next year's show. Efforts initially centred on an existing design – the P10. This was a double overhead-camshaft parallel twin, but after several months development it was apparent that the machine would prove to be too heavy, too rough and potentially too unreliable.

With only some three months to go before the show, engineering director Dr Stefan Bauer argued that conventional frame design was contrary to good engineering principles, and suggested that the P10 should have a frame based on a single top tube. Bauer also insisted that engine vibration could not be tolerated – and it was vibration that was one of the chief complaints with the existing Norton twins.

The idea put forward was completely radical – fit a modified version of the tried-and-tested Atlas engine to a new frame and to eliminate the problem of vibration, simply isolate the engine from the rider, together with the entire transmission train, including the rear wheel.

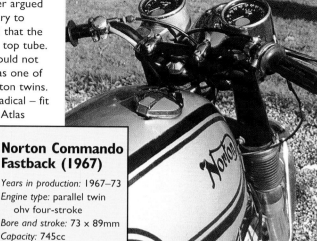

*This model, one of the first ten made, is finished in conventional Norton silver with red and black striping, a far cry from the colourful show machine.*

### Norton Commando Fastback (1967)

*Years in production:* 1967–73
*Engine type:* parallel twin
  ohv four-stroke
*Bore and stroke:* 73 x 89mm
*Capacity:* 745cc
*Compression ratio:* 8.9:1
*Power:* 58bhp @ 6500rpm
*Carburettors:* Amal
  concentric
*Tyres (front/rear):* 3 x 19in/
  3½ x 19in
*Wheelbase:* 56¾in
*Top speed:* 120mph

This was done by cleverly bolting the separate engine, gearbox and swinging-arm assembly together as one unit. The unit was suspended from a spine frame based on a 24in diameter top tube, using adjustable rubber bushes at three carefully calculated points. The idea worked superbly, allowing the engine to shake to its heart's content without disturbing the rider, and in 1969 the idea won an award for the most significant contribution to motorcycling.

Styling on the prototype was carried out by design consultants Wolf Ohlins, a company with no motorcycling experience. It included a silver frame and tank. At the rear it featured a ray hump, which led to the model being dubbed the 'Fastback'.

Much lighter than its predecessors, the machine had phenomenal acceleration for its day, under five seconds to reach 60mph, leading to a top speed of nearly 120mph.

*Fastback styling took the motorcycle world by storm in 1967. A forward angled engine, fibre-glass seat tail, and 'ears' coming forward from the seat to embrace the tank all hinted at the 120mph performance of which the machine was capable.*

# Norton P11

Norton's P11 'desert sled' was one of the British industry's inspired compromises. Something of a 'parts-bin special' it was a mix-and-match combination of parts from Norton and parent company AMC, designed to suit the American market and originally for export only. The result was so good that the few that found their way onto British roads, rapidly achieved cult status. With the enormous popularity of powerful, off-road twins that began in the 1980s, it can be seen as a machine that was way ahead of its time.

The P11 pre-dated Norton's more famous Commando, but in many ways it shared similar reasons for existence. The firm's Dominator twins had been developed to the limit while – despite the pedigree of its Featherbed frame– their 750cc derivative the Atlas was starting to look its age. With the cutbacks becoming a necessity in the mid 1960s, AMC was keen to reduce model variations and dispose of stock.

America still formed a big part of the market, where leisure motorcycling was far more significant than in Britain. Off-road sport in particular had long been an important sales area, and it was this that led to the launch of the P11. AMC's US distributor suggested that it might be possible to construct a machine especially for the popular West Coast desert races. AMC's Matchless G85CS had satisfied just such a market. Essentially a racing 500cc engine in a lightweight scrambler frame, it had been very successful, but was being outpowered. And so the P11 was born.

The Atlas engine together with the lightweight Matchless frame produced a brutal power to weight ratio. The tank was as small as practicable and made of alloy. Mudguards, silencer, side panels and other fittings followed suit. Everything was built for one purpose only – winning. Win it did. In its intended home of the Mojave desert the P11 reigned supreme in the closing years of the 1960s.

That same power could get out of hand on the road, where with off-road tyres and a short wheelbase its handling was not always as sure as expected.

Any criticism of its road performance missed the point, for no scrambler was equipped to deal with a performance of well over 100mph on the tarmac.

## Norton P11 (1969)

*Years in production:* 1967–69
*Engine type:* 360 degree
    parallel twin ohv four-stroke
*Bore and stroke:* 73 x 89mm
*Capacity:* 745cc
*Compression ratio:* 7.5:1
*Power:* 50bhp @ 6000rpm
*Carburettors:* twin Amal
    Concentrics
*Weight:* 380lb
*Top speed:* 110mph

Lightweight, lean and purposeful, these machines were costly to build, because the Norton engine was a tight fit in the Matchless frame and needed special spacers to match up. Their schizophrenic existence was obvious from the fact that a near-identical model was sold as the Matchless N15CS. But whatever their identity, the package worked superbly well. When both models were discontinued in 1969 they had already become a legend.

*Conceived as a racer first and foremost, in the late 1960s Norton's 'desert sled' took first place in California's Mojave desert for two years running. The powerful, lightweight package that resulted became a cult roadster.*

# Norton Commando (Roadster)

The Norton Commando was well placed to exploit the dawning of the superbike era and it enjoyed a healthy level of sales right from the start. In 1969 a MkII version was introduced, along with the Commando S model, which had high-level exhausts, both running down the left of the machine, and the more conventionally styled Roadster.

The Commando was launched into competition right from the start, and it was not long before the 750 gained its first track success. It would go on to win a host of events and records, while the entry in the 1970 Production TT just missed a 110mph lap.

The 750 models continued until late 1973, with various styling and mechanical changes one of which included the bizarre Hi-Rider, which had extreme Chopper styling with ultra high-rise bars and a seat with an extended backrest. But there was also a near disastrous change – the disc brake was adopted for the first time.

The Combat engine was developed with the idea of improving the power and performance. It had a strengthened bottom end, hot cams, high compression and gas-flowed head. Although this seemed a good idea, it was almost fatal for the model. The overstressed main bearings frequently gave way after as few as 5000 miles, while oil leaks and damage from over-revving were depressingly common.

Retrospectively, the problems were cured by fitting a new type of main bearing and by lowering the compression ratio, but the Combat engine had been an expensive folly.

However the 750 had some spectacular racing successes in the hands of Norton's brilliant rider-developer Peter Williams. With an isolastic frame, and a highly efficient fairing, Williams won the 1973 Formula 750 TT with the fastest lap of 107.57mph.

The 750cc MkV models were phased out in late 1973 to be replaced by the MkI 850cc which had appeared earlier in that year and would continue in production until 1975. By that time they had gained electric starting and numerous modifications all aimed at helping the Commando to compete with the reliability and performance of its competition – chiefly the new generation of Japanese superbikes.

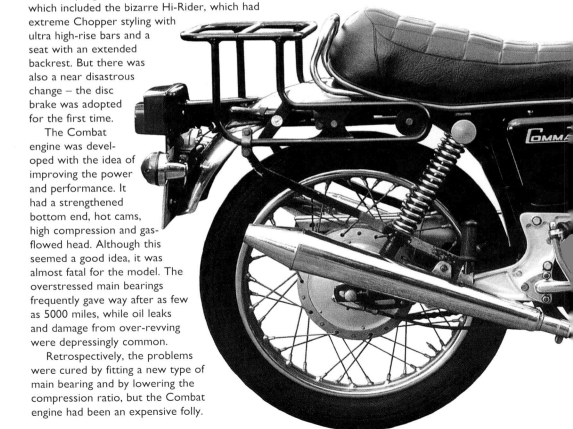

Sadly, by this time the parent company's financial difficulties and the problems of manufacture on worn, old machinery made it increasingly difficult to compete. While the machines were rightly loved by a generation of owners, it had to be acknowledged that running a Commando required a level of dedication and sympathy far higher than that demanded by a Honda or Kawasaki. And for Norton it would prove impossible to compete in selling what was effectively one design to a tiny proportion of the market. Despite its proud heritage and record, the Commando succumbed to old age and market pressures, with a final trickle of machines in 1978. Although the Norton name would live on in the form of the rotary-engined machines built at Shenstone in Staffordshire, the Commando marked the end of a line that had begun a long way back in the pioneer era.

## Norton Commando Roadster (1973)

*Years in production:* 1967–73 (750)
   1973–78 (850)
*Engine type:* parallel twin ohv four-stroke
*Bore and stroke:* 73 x 89mm (750)
   77 x 89mm (850)
*Capacity:* 745cc (750) 829cc (850)
*Compression ratio:* 9:1 (750)
   10:1 (Combat) 8.5:1 (850)
*Power:* 60bhp (750) 68bhp (Combat)
   60bhp @ 6000rpm (850) (claimed)
*Carburettors:* 30mm Amal Concentrics
   32mm (Combat and 850)
*Tyres (front/rear):* 4⅛ x 19in
*Top speed:* 125mph (claimed)

*Like the other later variants of the Commando, the Roadster was conventionally styled compared to its predecessors. Refinements included flashing indicators and a front disc broke. The disastrous 'improvement' of the over-tuned Combat engine was abandoned in 1973, the year of this 750cc MkV model.*

# Triumph Trident

The Triumph Trident began as part of the same development process as the BSA Rocket 3, but it was the Triumph that really proved the concept.

The first version of the Trident had an upright engine in a frame based on the single downtube Bonneville, quite unlike the BSA's angled engine and duplex frame, which meant that most of the major castings were different. By contrast to the BSA's radical styling, Triumph's version, the T150 Trident, had a family likeness to the contemporary twin, especially after a redesign in 1972.

The Trident sold much better than the Rocket 3, and about 45,000 were made, despite oil leaks and electrical faults. The drum brakes initially used were weak for a machine with such high performance, and had to be modified, although discs were fitted to later models.

*The T150 version of the Trident (above) has an upright engine, like the upright Triumph twin on which it was based. The frame has a single downtube similar to the twin's, and unlike the BSA version of the triples.*

The engine, too, needed heavy repairs over a lengthy running-in period. Fortunately the unconventional crank, eventually proved strong enough to last throughout the model's production life and to cope with uprated power outputs of around 100bhp.

There was a much happier story in competition, triples won most of the important short-circuit competitions, as well as taking the first three places in the 1971 Production TT.

## Triumph Trident T160 (1974)

*Years in production:* 1969–74 (T150) 1974 (T160)
*Engine type:* three-cylinder ohv four-stroke
*Bore and stroke:* 67 x 70mm
*Capacity:* 740cc
*Compression ratio:* 9.5:1
*Power:* 58bhp @ 7250rpm
*Gearbox:* four-speed in unit 32mm (Combat and 850)
*Tyres (front/rear):* 4⅛ x 19in
*Wheelbase:* 58in
*Weight:* 525lb
*Top speed:* 115mph

In Rocket 3 form, the triples' styling had already veered to the flamboyant, but in 1972 it was taken to excess with a model styled by the young American designer Craig Vetter. Planned as a limited edition model to appeal to American tastes, it was called the X75 Hurricane, and blended a stripped flat-track racer with the chopper styling brought into vogue by the recent film *Easy Rider*. Considered outrageous at the time, in hindsight it can be seen to have had an enormous effect on motorcycle styling.

From 1974 Triumph offered a new and much more conventional triple, the T160, using a version of the BSA's inclined engine. Variants of this model found their way on to the British market as the Cardinal. They were in fact part of a batch that had been destined for police use in the Middle East, but redirected when the deal fell through. This was effectively the end of the design. There had been plans to launch a 900cc version, as well as a 1000cc four, but the imminent financial collapse of the parent company, forced Triumph to concentrate on the much simpler twins.

*The final version of the Trident owed a great deal to the BSA Rocket 3, from which it borrowed the inclined engine. But unlike the heavy, over-styled BSA, the T160 was a lithe machine in the mould of previous generations of Triumph twins.*

# Rickman Enfield Interceptor

The Rickman Interceptor mated one of the biggest engines produced by the British industry to one of the best frames. Much lighter than its forebears, it had better handling and one of the first effective disc brakes. It should have been a splendid success, but in reality it represented a glorious swan song for one of the industry's great pioneers.

By the late 1960s the Rickman brothers Don and Derek were firmly established as makers of high-quality frames for sports machines, off-roaders and even police bikes. As Rickman began their rise, so Royal Enfield began to sink. Their flagship, the 750 Interceptor, had been launched in 1963, but the company was already in financial trouble.

The company's new owners had launched an ambitious programme, but further cutbacks followed, and the old Redditch works closed in 1966. The once-popular 250 singles ceased manufacture, and production of Interceptor frames was farmed out to Velocette. The company became part of the Norton Villiers group in 1967. Velocette now took over the spares operation, which they ran until they themselves closed in 1971.

Interceptors continued to be made throughout this period, although there was a gap between 1965 and 1967, when the model reappeared as the Series 1A. In 1968 the Series II model was launched.

Substantially different from the earlier machines, powerful and generally reliable, they were offered in an American styling with high bars that made hard work of the high top speeds.

Around 1000 engines were made when Royal Enfield ceased trading. Several hundred surplus power units were bought by the American Floyd Clymer, who launched the Indian Enfield 750 in America from 1969. The remaining batch went to Rickman, who built their own design.

Styling was an odd mix of café racer and tourer with high-rise bars clamped to the fork stanchions. Despite their quality and an excellent performance, the bikes were hampered by a high price as well as reservations about the engine and, particularly, the gearbox. Sales were slow, and under 140 were built in two years. Despite that, their charm and rarity ensured that they rate as one of the true classics from the declining British industry, while the survival of the Enfield name was a timely reminder of a firm that had helped to bring about its birth.

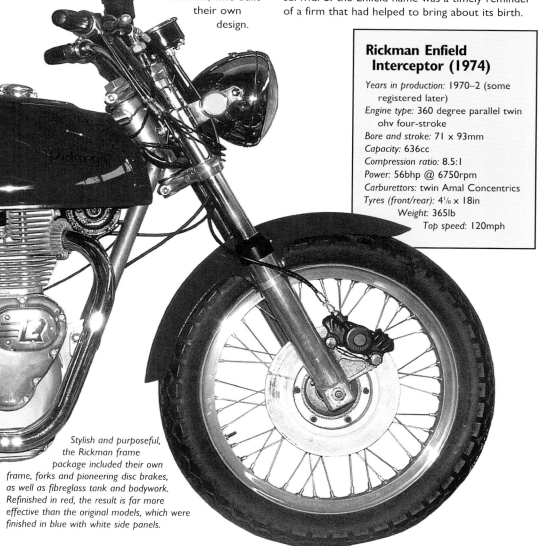

### Rickman Enfield Interceptor (1974)

*Years in production:* 1970–2 (some registered later)
*Engine type:* 360 degree parallel twin ohv four-stroke
*Bore and stroke:* 71 x 93mm
*Capacity:* 636cc
*Compression ratio:* 8.5:1
*Power:* 56bhp @ 6750rpm
*Carburettors:* twin Amal Concentrics
*Tyres (front/rear):* 4$\frac{1}{8}$ x 18in
*Weight:* 365lb
*Top speed:* 120mph

*Stylish and purposeful, the Rickman frame package included their own frame, forks and pioneering disc brakes, as well as fibreglass tank and bodywork. Refinished in red, the result is far more effective than the original models, which were finished in blue with white side panels.*

# Silk 700

In the mid 1970s the Silk gained a reputation for being one of the best handling machines of the day – although its reliability and out-right speed never attracted quite the same eulogies. It might have been unfair to expect any more, for the Silk, built by a small specialist engineering company based in Derbyshire, was a direct descendant of the venerable Scott two-stroke.

Company founder George Silk, a precision engineer who rode and tuned vintage Scotts in the 1960s. At the end of the decade, he set up Silk Engineering and offered a repair and parts service for Scotts including modifications and improvements. The chief of which was a frame offering a modern concept much closer to Alfred Scott's original ideas than anything in the previous 30 years. The frame, a product of nearby Spondon Engineering, was light and stiff with modern suspension at both ends. Spondon made their own forks and brakes too – and the whole package could easily be adapted to the engine that Silk was building.

*Recognisably a derivative of the 70-year-old Scott design, Silk's water-cooled two-stroke twin was far from being outclassed in the technology stokes by the Japanese competition. But the lack of investment required for true volume production meant that it was ultimately doomed to remain a specialist item.*

The radiator was either a Scott-type or borrowed from an LE Velocette, and the final piece in this most British of jigsaws was the gearbox – based on the late Velocette four-speed design, modified to allow it to be a built in unit with the engine. The 20 Scott-based Silk Specials constructed by 1975 were just that; specials built as a blend of many disparate components.

With assistance from some of Britain's foremost engineering specialists the Scott-based engine was substantially redesigned, with a patented scavenging system backed up by specially developed silencers, resulting in a smooth, powerful engine with good fuel economy. Other modern

## Silk 700 (1978)

*Years in production:* 1975–79
*Engine type:* twin-cylinder water cooled two-stroke
*Bore and stroke:* 76 x 72mm
*Capacity:* 653cc
*Compression ratio:* 8.5:1 (Mk II)
*Power:* 54bhp @ 6000rpm (Mk II)
*Gearbox:* four-speed
*Weight:* 309lb

features, such as state-of-the-art electronic ignition, were designed in from the start.

The result of all this was the Silk 700S – a proper production machine with parts manufactured by Silk or its suppliers. In a time when superbikes were becoming heavier, the most attractive feature of the 700S was its very absence of weight. With the Spondon frame, the handling was superb with good acceleration. Producing such a machine in small numbers was difficult and Silk found the going hard at a time when most of the British industry was collapsing. There was no way in which the Silk could have attracted a mass market or financed volume production. Fewer than 150 were built.

# Triumph T140 Bonneville

The Triumph Bonneville was a survivor. Clearly based on Edward Turner's pre-war concept, it upheld traditional values while adopting the modern conveniences demanded by a new generation. Despite a number of obvious shortcomings, it won admirers throughout the superbike era.

The last of the long line of Triumph twins had an inauspicious beginning, when its launch was delayed by design problems. It began in 1971, in 650cc form with a new frame heavily based on the BSA A65, sharing its oil-in-frame design, with similar short-comings as a result of an excessively high seat. By now, 'mod-cons' such as indicators were the norm, but with its drum brakes and kick-start, the T120 Bonneville was years behind the Honda 750 Four launched three years earlier. Vibration and oil consumption were also a problem, but even the Japanese competition could not match the handling.

The first 750cc versions appeared the following year as the T140V. Essentially, this was a bored-out 650 and, apart from minor variations, it shared the smaller bike's cycle parts, which now included a new front disc brake. The first few models were 724cc, but this soon settled at 744cc with a slightly larger bore. More softly tuned than the 650, the engine was also strength-ened, with more positive location

for the head and an extra holding-down stud; the transmission was beefed up, and there were other detail changes.

The parallel twin's vibration was worse on the new model, and it was slow to gain acceptance, especially while the 650cc ran alongside it. Worse still, the Meridien factory's problems reached a head late in 1973, ultimately resulting in the workers' occupation. No new machines appeared until mid 1974, and those that did emerge showed evidence of hasty finishing. The following year matters improved as the workers' cooperative got underway and settled down to doing what they knew best. Existing machines were sold off to make way for a new model, with an engine that had been modified to suit the American market's insistence on a left-foot gearchange – a regulation that was introduced in 1974.

## Triumph T140 Bonneville (1978)

*Years in production:* 1973–88
*Engine type:* twin-cylinder ohv
  four-stroke
*Bore and stroke:* 76 x 82mm
*Capacity:* 744cc
*Compression ratio:* 7.9:1
*Power:* 49bhp @ 6500rpm
*Carburettors:* Two 30mm Amal
  Concentrics
*Gearbox:* five-speed
*Tyres (front/rear):* 4¹⁄₈ x 19in/ 4¹⁄₈ x 18in
*Weight:* 395lb
*Top speed:* 111mph

# Endings and Beginnings

Quality control proved a problem with antiquated machinery and limited funds, but by 1977 the factory was able to offer a limited edition Jubilee model, to mark the Queen's Silver Jubilee. With a number of minor refinements introduced in 1978, the T140, as the model was now styled, had become a reasonably sound, if anachronistic, option.

The year 1979 brought the launch of the T140E and the T140D, a custom special. Around 20,000 machines based on the new design were built before Triumph finally went to the wall. These included an 'executive' tourer, the first electric start model, an economy 650

version, a trail variant and finally the eight-valve TSS and custom TSX.

The Meridien cooperative went into liquidation in 1982 and the assets were bought by John Bloor who assigned limited rights to build the Bonneville to Les Harris's Devon based company. Harris built a limited number of Bonnies between 1985 and 1988, but although this spelt the end for the old twin, by then Bloor's own plans to write a new chapter in the Triumph story were well advanced.

*Old world charm for the new world: American specification features include high bars and traditional streamlined Triumph tank. The simple controls and instruments show little concession to the ergonomics which were starting to dominate design thinking in the 1970s.*

*The traditional virtues of Triumph's 750cc twin included light weight, simplicity and good handling. But there were few concessions to the contemporary world of superbikes, with the exception of a front disc brake and flashing indicators.*

# Hesketh Vampire

By the late 1970s it was obvious to all that the British industry had been in terminal decline for a long time. So when it leaked out that someone was preparing to invest substantially in a completely new model, it was greeted with enthusiasm from many sides.

The man behind the machine was Lord Hesketh, a fully fledged baron with an impressive estate in Northamptonshire. In 1973 Hesketh, then aged just 22, ran a Formula One car-racing team and in 1975 came fourth in the World Championship. Financially, however, things were not going well and in 1974 Hesketh decided to develop a motorcycle to capitalise on his racing record and supplement the company's income.

## Hesketh Vampire (1984)

*Years in production:* 1982-83
*Engine type:* four-valve 90 degree V-twin four-stroke
*Bore and stroke:* 95 x 70mm
*Capacity:* 992cc
*Compression ratio:* 10.5:1
*Carburettors:* 36mm Amal MkII Concentric/Dell'Orto PHFs
*Wheelbase:* 59½in
*Weight:* 506lb (V1000) 544lb (Vampire)
*Top speed:* 120mph

*Impressive instrumentation (right) included a clock and a gauge to show the ambient temperature. Hydraulic operation for the clutch was a Hesketh innovation.*

Several ideas were floated, including buying the near defunct Norton factory or making frame kits for Japanese bikes. But motorcycle sales were enjoying a boom and European twins were growing in popularity. In 1977, Hesketh began talks with engine specialists Weslake that would result in the development of the company's own 1000cc V-twin, a classically British type of engine that was proving to be a great success for Ducati.

Unfortunately the project soon ran into trouble, much of the trouble stemming from the conflicting demands of Hesketh's largely car-based team of designers with Weslake's own engineers. But restrictions on the design meant there had to be many compromises.

*Heavy and tall, the Vampire was a last-ditch attempt to make a success out of the failed Hesketh V1000 by turning it into a tourer. But the fairing offered inadequate protection, and the bike still suffered from the basic deficiencies caused by a lack of development. Few sold, and the company foundered for a second time in the early 1980s.*

Despite the problems, an enthusiastic press launch went ahead in the spring of 1980. The bike was traditionally styled, with a small cockpit fairing and handsomely plated frame. Its layout was similar to the contemporary Ducati 90 degree 'L-twin', although at over 500 lb, its chunky looks were a world away from the lithe Italian. As no existing factory was able to take on quantity manufacture, Hesketh set up his own at Daventry and the process of V1000 production began.

In 1981 press reports criticised the clunky gearchange, engine noise, handling and price. Urgent revisions were put in hand, but Hesketh was short of money and only 100 or so were sold before the company was wound up in August 1982.

The postscript was not long in following. Hesketh and partners had formed a new firm, to sell a package of modifications for the existing machines, at the same time developing a new fully faired tourer, the Vampire. But the gearbox faults, which included a host of false neutrals, persisted, while the engine was noisy and the fairing restricted the turning circle without giving adequate protection. After a couple of years only a handful had been sold, and there were further lay-offs. While members of the enthusiastic team continued their own development work, it was the end for Hesketh himself and yet another last hope for the British industry.

*The unfaired V1000 (left): the massive Hesketh engine – the cause of most of the troubles – was slung from a simple, plated tube frame. Problems included oil leaks from the chain-cases to the overhead-camshafts, heavy vibration and a lumpy gearchange, despite a low state of tune.*

# Norton Wankel Rotary

Although it ended up wearing a Norton badge, the British rotary spent years being batted about between the various company groups that formed as the industry went into terminal decline. But the Norton rotary was a brave effort by a small and dedicated team that added an important chapter to the story of the British motorcycle.

The Wankel engine was invented by Germany's Dr Felix Wankel, who took a first patent on the principle in the late 1920s. It was not until the late 1950s that the engine was used in some NSU cars, notably the Ro80.

The Wankel's advantages seemed numerous: doing away with the moving parts of a conventional piston engine, and replacing them with a simple rotor offered incredible smoothness. Unfortunately, it was not that simple, with problems arising from the complexity of sealing and lubricating the rotor.

Rotary-engined machines appeared throughout the 1970s, including motorcycles from Suzuki, Hercules/DKW, Van Veen Kriedler and a prototype Yamaha. Only the Suzuki RE5 succeeded, but it proved too heavy and thirsty to become anything more than a curiosity. The only company to make much of a success of the concept was Mazda with the RX7 sports car.

Among the other experimenters was the BSA group, at that time a massive conglomerate with extensive R&D facilities. Using a proprietary German engine with a single rotor and fan cooling, an experimental machine was built in 1969. Having identified several problem areas, BSA built its own

*The unconventional shape of Norton's air-cooled twin-rotor engine (above) harks back to a prototype developed by BSA as early as 1971. The concept was originally developed by Dr Felix Wankel, working for NSU in Germany.*

prototype in 1970, using an air-cooled twin-rotor layout, and a year later came up with an idea that greatly improved cooling efficiency.

As the decade wore on, BSA's increasing financial difficulties led to cutbacks, but the programme was still alive as BSA was taken over by the Norton-Villiers-Triumph group. Prototypes were tested in 1974, but a year later NVT collapsed.

The rotary project was salvaged from the collapse and given to a small but expert team based at Shenstone in Staffordshire. Their work bore fruit in the early 1980s when several police forces and the armed forces took delivery of the Interpol 11. In 1987, the company launched the limited edition unfaired Classic, designed to test the market. At the end of the year, the fully-equipped Commander, with a liquid-cooled version of the engine, was launched to many plaudits, despite its premium price and rather high fuel consumption.

*Behind its fairing, the Commander concealed a liquid-cooled version of the twin-rotor engine developing 85 bhp, propelling the tourer to around 125mph. The panniers were initially integral with the body-work. The brakes, like the front wheel, were culled from the XJ900 Yamaha.*

## Norton Wankel Rotary

*Years in production:* 1987 (Classic)
*Engine type:* twin-rotor air-cooled
  rotary
*Capacity:* 588cc
*Compression ratio:* 7.5:1
*Power:* 79bhp @ 9000rpm
*Carburettor:* 1½in constant vacuum
*Tyres (front/rear):* 100/90 V18/
  120/80 V18
*Wheelbase:* 58½in
*Weight:* 498lb
*Top speed:* 120mph

*Classic Norton: the unfaired silver machine with red and black coachlining designed to recall traditional values.*

A prototype racer was also developed and when this finally took to the track it showed enormous potential although there was a dispute as to whether its unconventional engine should be classified as a 588cc, as Norton claimed, or much more. Eventually the governing bodies settled on a formula that enabled it to compete as a 1000cc machine. By the end of the decade, with new sponsors JPS, the Nortons had won the British Formula One and Shell Supercup, and the Norton name was seen on a TT leaderboard for the first time since 1973.

From then on the Norton story became a bitter tale of dedicated engineers producing a trickle of motorcycles, against a backdrop of a financial confusion. However it may be premature to draw a line under the Norton story; after 100 years in production, it is perhaps to be hoped that the firm may see its rebirth as a major force in the same way as Triumph.

# Triumph Trident

The reborn, modern Triumph is a machine that can hold its head up with the best in the world. The marque proved Britain could still produce a world-class motorcycle manufacturer after so many 'new British world-beaters' had foundered. Triumph has prospered by adopting the design traditions of the very Japanese machines that had helped to kill off the British bike. Triumph had come to an end with the collapse of the Meridien cooperative in 1981. But there were those who believed that the Triumph name still had something going for it – its thousands of devoted owners and enthusiasts. It was these people that the new owner of the Triumph name was counting on, when a new company suddenly emerged at the end of the 1980s.

**Triumph Trident (1995)**

*Engine type:* liquid-cooled double
    overhead-cam in-line three-
    cylinder
*Bore and stroke:* 76 x 65mm
*Capacity:* 885cc
*Compression ratio:* 10.6:1
*Power:* 98bhp @ 9000rpm
*Carburettors:* 3x36mm flat slide
    constant vacuum
*Tyres (front/rear):* 120/70 ZR17/
    180/55 ZR17
*Wheelbase:* 58½in

*This unfaired touring Trident demonstrates the essence of the Hinckley Triumph concept. Recognisably modern and owing much to the Japanese tradition, the three-cylinder engine is in a class of its own*

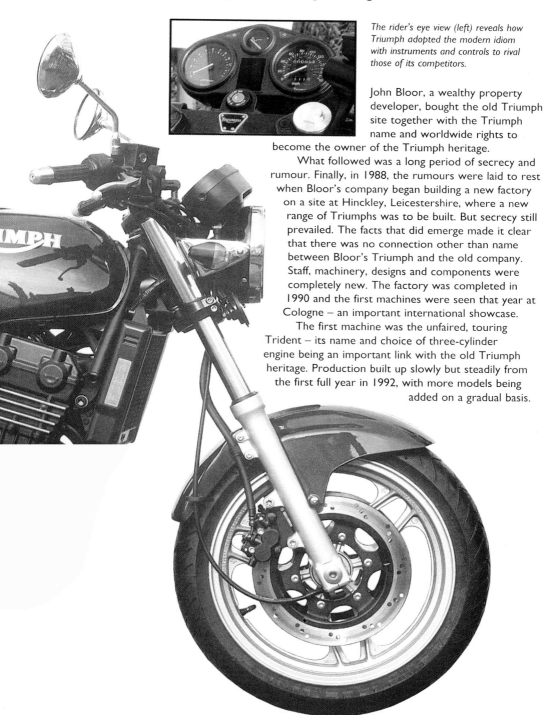

The rider's eye view (left) reveals how Triumph adopted the modern idiom with instruments and controls to rival those of its competitors.

John Bloor, a wealthy property developer, bought the old Triumph site together with the Triumph name and worldwide rights to become the owner of the Triumph heritage.

What followed was a long period of secrecy and rumour. Finally, in 1988, the rumours were laid to rest when Bloor's company began building a new factory on a site at Hinckley, Leicestershire, where a new range of Triumphs was to be built. But secrecy still prevailed. The facts that did emerge made it clear that there was no connection other than name between Bloor's Triumph and the old company. Staff, machinery, designs and components were completely new. The factory was completed in 1990 and the first machines were seen that year at Cologne – an important international showcase.

The first machine was the unfaired, touring Trident – its name and choice of three-cylinder engine being an important link with the old Triumph heritage. Production built up slowly but steadily from the first full year in 1992, with more models being added on a gradual basis.

# Triumph T595 Daytona

As the millennium approached, it was becoming clear what class of bike would rule the roost in the late 1990s. Sports bikes, as epitomised by Ducati's 916 and Honda's hi-tech Fireblade, were the machines that grabbed the headlines. For a new manufacturer like Triumph to compete at this level, a machine was needed that was both distinctively different and able to deliver the goods – no small undertaking for such a new company.

The solution was the T595 Daytona, which rapidly established itself as a bike with the capability to beat the best on the track as well as being a supremely usable street machine. Based on Triumph's trademark triple engine, it was an all-new 955cc design developed with the Lotus car race engineers. The object of the exercise was to optimise porting, valve and combustion chamber shapes, improving breathing. Stronger components

ensured reliability at higher engine speeds and out-puts, while new materials for non-stress-bearing components saved weight.

The engine management system, claimed to be the most complex and smartest ever fitted. The full-power version gave 128bhp at 10,200rpm, with a massive 74 ft lb of torque peaking at 8,500rpm. Matching the new engine was a new twin-spar perimeter frame that offered a radical departure, made from aluminium extrusions. With a single-sided swinging arm and Japanese Showa suspension, handling was impeccable, while wheels, tyres and brakes were to the highest specification.

Versatility was one of the objectives, aimed at providing the ultimate street bike as well as offering race-winning potential. The tucked-in silencer could easily be replaced with a full race component, while the sophisticated frame and forks were well up to the 160mph-plus potential of the stock machine.

Triumph also offered a stripped version of the same machine, the T509 Speed Triple, which had a slightly lower performance. Together, both machines demonstrated the technical capabilities of the new Triumph factory and showed that the British industry had fully shaken off its past problems to face a new era of motorcycling.

*The slimline fairing with twin headlamps (above) offers the height of contemporary styling but conceals the hi-tech aluminium frame, the twin spars of which snake over the top of the three-cylinder power unit.*

*The distinctive three-spoke alloy wheels were designed by Triumph and produced in Italy especially for this model. The brakes, sourced in Japan, use four piston cappers with floating discs. The tucked-in silencer, designed to take advantage of the single-sided rear suspension, can be replaced with a racing unit.*

## Triumph T595 Daytona (1997)

*Years in production:* 1996–
*Engine type:* double overhead-cam
    four-stroke four-valve in-line triple
*Bore and stroke:* 79 x 65mm
*Capacity:* 955cc
*Compression ratio:* 11.2:1
*Fuel system:* Sagem fuel injection
*Power:* 128bhp @ 10,200rpm
*Transmission:* six-speed gearbox
*Top speed:* 161 mph

# Triumph Thunderbird

Although factory founder John Bloor had ridden a motorcycle in his youth, he was far from being one of the many passionate enthusiasts who had tried to revive the British industry in the 1970s. As a hard-headed and successful businessman, he knew the value of brand loyalty and recognised the potential asset represented by such a well-respected name as Triumph.

Although the Triumph logo itself had been subtly redesigned, it was recognisably the same as the one that had graced the best-loved models in the company's history. Similarly, there were echoes of the old Triumph in the choice of a basic three-cylinder engine, and in the choice of the model names. With the average Hinckley Triumph buyer approaching 40 years of age, such historic resonances might be expected to strike a chord.

## Triumph Thunderbird (1995)

*Engine type:* liquid-cooled double overhead cam in-line three-cylinder four-stroke
*Bore and stroke:* 76 x 65mm
*Capacity:* 885cc
*Compression ratio:* 10.6:1
*Power:* 70bhp @ 8000rpm
*Carburettors:* 3 x 36mm flat slide constant vacuum
*Tyres (front/rear):* 110/80 18/160/80 16
*Wheelbase:* 58½in

*With a tank, seat and mudguards which echo the styling of twins from Triumph's heyday, the Thunderbird proved an instant hit.*